*A Spiritu

THE UNIVERSAL LAWS *of* AWAKENING

Tonya Kinlow

Copyright © 2022 Tonya Kinlow

All rights reserved. No part of this publication in print or in electronic format may be reproduced, stored in a retrieval system, or transmitted in any form or by any means, electronic, mechanical, photocopying, recording, or otherwise without the prior written permission of the publisher.

The scanning, uploading, and distribution of this book without permission is a theft of the author's intellectual property. Thank you for your support of the author's rights.

Distribution by Bublish, Inc.
Published by TK Inspirations

TKI REMARKABLE WELLNESS
DISCOVERING HEALTH THROUGH PURPOSE

ISBN: 978-1-647046-12-5 (eBook)
ISBN: 978-1-647046-13-2 (paperback)

DEDICATION

To Mom and Dad—you are wonderful parents.

If I had ten thousand tongues, I couldn't thank you enough. I go within for the words and sit with God.

He told me the truth is simple, and so I end where I started: perfected by His grace...

I love you.

*Whoever you are, or whatever it is that you do,
When you really want something,
it's because that desire originated in the soul of the Universe...
And when you want something,
all the Universe conspires in helping you achieve it.*

The Alchemist

CONTENTS

Introduction ix

PART ONE: AWAKENING

The Dream of My Box 7
The Questions 11
Limitlessness 13
Understanding Divine Intelligence 19
    Belief 22
    Meditation and Prayer 24
    The Fabric of Belief 26
    The Mind 28
    All Is One in Consciousness 31
Universal Laws of Order & Design 35

PART TWO: THE UNIVERSAL LAWS OF AWAKENING

The Universal Laws of Awakening 41

Law 1:   The Law of Love & Fear 46
Law 2:   The Law of One 52
Law 3:   The Law of Relationship 56
Law 4:   The Law of Polarity 66
Law 5:   The Law of the Pendulum 76
Law 6:   The Law of Vibration 82
Law 7:   The Law of Giving & Receiving 88
Law 8:   The Law of Ebb & Flow 94

Law 9: The Law of Silence 102
Law 10: The Law of Dimensionality 106
Law 11: The Law of Self-Actualization 114

PART THREE: THE BODY AND THE WORLD

The Body and the World 123

The Body 125
The World 129
Healing 131
A Cautionary Tale 137

PART FOUR: THE WAY

Awakening: The Spiritual Journey 147

Practical Practices for Awakening 155
   The Spiritual Scientific Method 156
   The Seven Intentions 160

PART FIVE: GO IN PEACE - NEXT STEPS

Acknowledgements 169

INTRODUCTION

My father, a Pentecostal preacher, told me that *something major* happens in everyone's life around the age of forty. I didn't know what he was talking about at the time, but now I know he has never been more right. For me, the pressure started to build in my mid-thirties and then simply exploded when I was forty. I wish my father had told me more specifically what *something major* meant and how to navigate it. But now I understand, and I can share my wisdom to ease the way for others during their season of uncertainty.

I used the lessons I learned from my upbringing. I leaned into my faith, prayed, tried to be a good person, and trusted God. Still, everything seemed to be working against me over a span of four years. I was peppered with a health problems, life and death decisions for my children, a horrible boss, and a difficult divorce.

Most of us develop our understanding of the world through our upbringing or religion. We look at things through the lens we were taught to look through. My life had provided me with the lessons of how to thrive and function as a responsible citizen of the world but had not taught me how to *be happy*. In my most dire time of need, my life skills failed me. What was wrong with me?

I remember being jolted out of my sleep in the middle of the night by the sharp pain of despair. I sat straight up and just wailed for hours. I couldn't understand why everything was so messed up.

Have you experienced a moment like this? You know, a moment when you ask yourself, "What is the point of all this? What am I doing wrong? Why is the world so unjust? Who am I?"

I discovered this earnest questioning marks the beginning of the *something major* my dad had told me about. It is referred to as the dark night of the soul, but it is life's call to *Awaken*. It marks the soul's season of expansion from the material to the spiritual. It is like the moment a seed bursts through the soil into the light or a butterfly emerges from the cocoon and flies. It is a change we all resist but must overcome to achieve transformation. Don't take it personally; it is *universal*.

The Universal Laws of Awakening is a complete introduction to transformation. If you sincerely want to understand the world in a way that supports the spiritual Awakening of your soul's purpose, and if you intend to earnestly practice and pursue this aim, then you have found this book for a reason. Wouldn't it be wonderful if we each possessed the mystical secrets of the universe to fix the problems in our lives, sparing ourselves countless tears and years of suffering? What if I told you that we do? The information is in hand. The Universal Laws remind us that we have everything we need within us and gives instructions for how to let the answers we seek emerge as our primary function instead of feeling like we're in a knife fight with the devil and the devil has a gun.

Rumi, my favorite poet and philosopher, asks, "Why do you stay in prison when the door is wide open?" I believe it is because we look backward to the early life teachings that served us in our youth. However, these patterns do not work in maturity. Spiritual growth and purpose are the mark of the new human, and awareness and application are the way. When I was a child, I spoke as a child; when I grew up, I put childish things aside. *The Laws of the Universe* are all you need to turn around and see the new way, which is the *only* way, out of the prison of your mind.

In this book, you will learn eleven laws that explain the spiritual workings of the Universe. The Law of Vibration will teach you how to solve problems by changing your energy. The Law of the Pendulum and the Law of Ebb & Flow will teach you about various rhythms of the Universe and how to use those rhythms to your advantage.

Do not be overwhelmed. It is not necessary to commit all the laws to memory. These laws are so foundational that you only need to fully appreciate any one of them to attain the most important element that exists in all of them.

The Universal Laws of Awakening will teach you how to transcend beyond your current situation with wisdom and without guilt or shame. This is and has always been your functional design. The fact that you are reading these words right now indicates that you are exactly where you are meant to be and ready to receive direction to your soul's calling. The spiritual journey turns your life from one of survival to one of self-exploration and inner peace. This is the instructional wisdom I wish I'd had to midwife me through my troubles. It is the lighthouse to guide your way to Universal wisdom for your own transcendence. Engage with it and please, please, please give it to anyone who is going through *something major*.

Let's begin...

PART ONE

AWAKENING

Dear Beloved,

Your desire to understand the timing of events in your life and how to live a life of happiness and well-being has been heard. This book teaches that all problems are solved by the Laws of the Universe. Eleven of the primary laws are presented here, and they will immediately change your life when you use them in your decision-making.

The Universal Laws of Awakening is a gift to you from Consciousness. This wisdom comes to you at a critical time in the renaissance of the world's Awakening. You will find that reading this book in small doses provides massive restorative and enduring results. Be easy on yourself and take your time. Change takes energy.

As you Awaken to your significance in relation to all life, you grow and become a change agent for the entire world. Do not take this responsibility lightly. You are Divinely led to this moment. It is also important that you do *not* share this book with a mind not yet ripe for Awakening. Unexamined fears from others will cause delays in your own transformation. *The Universal Laws of Awakening* illuminates the place of peace that abides within you. And then, transcendence...

For the ears that can hear.

Love & Light,
TK

A person is the product of their dreams.
So make sure to dream great dreams.

Maya Angelou

THE DREAM OF MY BOX

Many years ago, I woke up one night very suddenly—heart pounding out of my chest as I sat straight up in bed—after a profound dream. Disoriented, I fumbled for focus. Even then, all I could do was grab at the dream I'd just had, which began the journey back to my True Self.

I dreamed I was in a box. My box was a mystical one, and somehow, I knew I'd been poured into the box by *The Great Author of All That Is* to keep me safe, comfortable, and happy. He had already written my story and supplied everything I needed and desired. My box had warmth and light and was created for me to experience love—and to *give* love. That is all. This box would expand until I had everything I enjoyed: adventure and awe, risk and reward, loyalty and passion, and most of all, *love*. It contained every craft and tool I would ever need. My life was the center of the Universe in this beautiful box. It was my personal vignette of heaven.

This was home—and it had windows that stretched from the floor to the sky, where the world's resplendent vistas surrounded me. When darkness came, I could see countless bright lights glittering like stars in the night sky. Somehow, I inherently knew they were other boxes, just like mine, experiencing what The Great Author had written for them. They looked fun and enticing, and it was hard to keep my eyes off them.

Every once in a while, I would open the windows of my box and let little pieces of my life experience float out, where they would attach themselves to other sparkling boxes, fly away, and eventually be forgotten. Other times, I would take the things somebody else released into the sky and hoard them for their beauty—things that looked like fine clothes, mansions, and exotic places. I coveted these bits and pieces from other boxes and tried to make them mine, thinking that I could, even though they had not been written for me.

After some time, my box was depleted of almost everything that originally came from The Great Author of All That Is. I had given it all away. My box had but a fraction of its original unique beauty, empty of the joy meant for me. Now, it was filled with other people's stuff. I had given away most of my own treasures. I realized the robust, rich density in my box had turned to vapor, and I could not find the essence of myself anymore.

All that was left of me was the shell of my box, and I felt alone. Everything that was meant for me and brought me joy had disappeared.

As I searched, I discovered that deep in the bowels of depression is the desperation to feel joy again. I took my grievances to The Great Author of All That Is, blamed Him for my misfortune, and asked Him to rewrite my story. This was His reply:

"My sweet, dear child. Your story cannot be changed, for it is already written with many possibilities. Try as you might to raise your fist and stomp your feet in demand, the way to fill your box to its original glory is your journey to take. You have *responsibility* and *agency* written and encoded within you that never change. It is the foundation of who you are. It does not live in the lives of others. So, pay attention.

"Your *agency* is expressed as free will and gives you degrees of freedom to stray from the story written for you. Your *responsibility* is to remember the truth of who you are and return to your own storyline. The further you stray, the longer the journey. Yet the truth does not change. It may take you a thousand lifetimes to learn the way, but I am The Great Author of All That Is, and you must follow this Universal wisdom to get back on your path.

"What you let in through the windows will never be of any real consequence to your story. Those things are just what they look like: items and instances of temporary happiness though infinite experience. But never get too attached to them because they are not yours. You are meant to catch and release. They are beautiful for you to gaze upon and appreciate, but only what is meant for you is for you. I promise, my love, your pieces will come back to you when you ask for them, because I always supply your needs. There is but one admonition: your pieces and blessings will only come to you through the lid of the box, as it was in the beginning, never through the windows."

And so, I called back all the pieces of me I had unwittingly given to others. I learned the windows are on the horizontal plane and therefore limit my full potential. When I focus on what is outside of my box, I forget the truth of what lies inside and lose my way. I learned my thoughts must *first* focus squarely on what is within to anchor me. I learned personal fulfillment is of the vertical plane and must be poured through the top of the box, as it was in the beginning. Only here exists the truth, wisdom, and abundance. The resources of The Great Author of All That Is can never be depleted.

I discovered my inner thoughts reveal my purpose to create my experiences in the outer world. And so, I continued to turn my vision upward and call my light back into myself, until I was once again strong, dense, and robust, filled with love and light. Soon my box grew so spectacularly that it merged with other boxes, until my joy was limitless. Like a cup of water poured into the ocean, my power increased as I shared the vast brilliance of the Universe. I learned what is in the whole is in the one and what is in the one is in the whole.

Suddenly, I was strong and loved and secure again. It is our purpose to live harmoniously and more abundantly, as written by The Great Author of All That Is.

And so, it is.

THE QUESTIONS

Is life a dream? Can happiness truly exist in the midst of chaos? Spirituality suggests that, yes, it is possible and teaches us the way. Yet, much of the wisdom for *how* to live this joyful experience has been obscured. We have come to rely on what our five senses can materially gain. Ironically, it is this reliance on the sensorium that limits our understanding of what happiness is and where it comes from. There is more out there, waiting to delight you in ways still beyond your imagination and definitely beyond what you can hear, see, smell, touch, or taste.

The true wisdom of the world has been lost through a collective amnesia. By opening our minds to the vastness of Reality beyond our five senses, we remember clearly why we are here and how to live happily with our very own existence. And because the Universe is kind and Consciousness is benevolent, we can relearn what has never changed. Everything is connected, and all is One.

By developing your own sixth sense of spirituality and Awakening to the power of Consciousness within you, the answers to the questions you seek can come quickly with earnest contemplation.

At the end of each introduction to a new law or concept, there will be questions to consider. Take ten to fifteen minutes to ask your Inner Self these questions and search for the answers based on the law just presented. Your consideration in each chapter is the personal experience that will open your mind to receive clarifying solutions at any point in time.

LIMITLESSNESS

A man of average build begins to run up a steep hill. After a while, he begins to slow down from exhaustion yet still makes progress. Eventually, his pace plateaus. This illustrates the concept of diminishing returns. Although the man is still running up the hill, his pace slows as he tires, and he covers less ground than he did when he first started. In our human evolution, we have reached the point of diminishing returns as it pertains to happiness. As hard as we try, we are less happy and cannot keep the current pace.

The quest for material gain cannot bring peace because it is inherently accompanied by open-ended expectations. If there is only more to gain, and never an end to the quest, then how can we reach peace? This is a cycle of madness that will only end when we commit to a new mindset, one which is dedicated to the nonmaterial. These are the treasures that will attract what you need for your life's purpose. Here is where happiness abides.

In Consciousness, there is no concept of diminishing returns. It is *limitless*. In the spirit, there are infinite possibilities and abundance and the peace that surpasses understanding. As we collectively Awaken to this truth, we open our minds to rediscover a spiritual technology that transforms us into our highest and best selves. With peace and joy being our primary purpose and focus, we relearn the Universal Laws that have been lost to us over the millennia.

In this book, you will be reintroduced to spiritual technology, the Universal Laws operating oneness, vibration, energy, balance, polarity, magnetism, cause and effect, giving and receiving, and more. As you learn to apply these laws in your life, you will unfold your awareness and the ultimate design of Reality, and your purpose will be revealed. Spiritual technology is built on the Universal Laws upon which every way is made possible. Through these principles, you will come to know you have everything you need to live harmoniously.

You cannot fail. *You lack nothing.*

...I am the unknown in the known
And the known in the unknown

I am the love in hatred
and the hope in despair

I am the same in all difference
And different in the same

I am the isness of things
And the amness of self...

>Rupert Spira, "I Am"

UNDERSTANDING DIVINE INTELLIGENCE

You likely experience most of life's wonders through your five physical senses. Yet the deepest wonders have no form at all—love, compassion, kindness, and the like—and so the greatest of life's gifts regularly go unnoticed. What do all things in existence have in common that gives them expression? How does your little body and the vast sun coexist? These questions dominate as life becomes more complicated because we have an innate need to feel grounded before we can fly. The answer is surprisingly simple. Everything has the same Source.

Just like air connects to and with all things but is not those things, the Source of all things is more fundamental. It gives everything the ability to express itself. It is that which even air needs to breathe. It is like the screen on which a movie plays or the page on which words are written. This foundation is critical to project the action or the words yet totally taken for granted during the experience.

The essence of all things rests in omnipresence, undetectable by the human eye and often ignored. It is this critical element of life to which you turn your attention for

Awakening. This essence of life is known as ether, a transparent, Divine fabric from which all things are created and in which all things exist as unique expressions. It is pure intelligence, truth, and light.

This all-knowing fabric is *Divine Intelligence,* and the Universal Laws are the threads that harmoniously hold all things together. Divine Intelligence contains the primordial code to existence itself. It operates within a space that is vast, transparent, still, and pure. We call this space Consciousness. Divine Intelligence and Consciousness coexist and together are literally *the stuff everything is made of.* Your spirit and everything in creation share this *sameness,* the building blocks for life.

Think of Consciousness as the movie screen. Divine Intelligence is the author of the story, and the Universal Laws structure the experience to bring everything into alignment for your enjoyment. The laws create a constant framework you can understand: a premise, a plot, a twist, a conflict, and a resolution. When this order is out of alignment with your expectations, you will not understand the story and will have a negative experience.

The more attention we give to the essential elements of the story, the more we connect with the content and experience the awareness of joy and contentment intended by the Great Author. We begin to see our connection with everything else and uncover meaning in our lives. From here on out, we spend increasingly more time understanding this space of luminosity, which makes the story that much better.

It is worth taking a moment here to point out that, as we expose the Universal Laws, there are many different expressions for the Great Author of All That Is. The Universe,

Source, Consciousness, Reality, and God are used herein to describe the *All* from a specific aspect as it pertains to the laws.

This is just like how a gold earring and a gold statue can be made from the same vat of gold yet their form and function give a unique expression of the gold's beauty. In this way, the best expression of the All will arise where it has its best function.

As you look at the illustrations for the laws, let yourself feel the meaning behind the words *creatively*. In your mind's eye, imagine an infinite expanse vaster than the skies from which everything flows, from which all knowledge exists, and in which all possibilities are experienced.

As we grow, we become *aware* of this expansive Consciousness within ourselves, even though it has always been there. This may feel like a desire for understanding and a striving for inner peace. Everything that is known can only be known with awareness. Your spark of inner questioning is the beginning to what we call *Awakening*. The journey of Awakening is what answers all questions and brings you to the truth of who you are.

Take a moment to turn your palms upward and feel the vibration emanating from them; you are not creating the Reality of that vibration. However, it is your awareness that allows you to experience the truth of your hand more intimately. The vibration is occurring whether you give it attention or not. Your true essence is pure energy and ever present. Reality exists as this state of being. Awareness of Divine Intelligence, just like bringing awareness to your hands, automatically brings with it clarity and wisdom. Wisdom can turn a sad thought into a happy thought, reduce the suffering of a headache, lighten the mood in a room, and at the highest level of devoted attention, cure sickness.

Consciousness is the creative platform on which the power-changing dynamic of life is at play. By making choices through the lens of Consciousness, you access Divine Intelligence and make the best decisions with Source knowledge. This is the direct path for spiritual Awakening. When you are unconscious, your awareness is like a pair of dirty eyeglasses that can only see problems.

You are an expression of Consciousness, and without awareness, you miss experiencing the miracles of life just as regularly as you overlook the vibration of your hands. Now you take this corollary as truth: *Reality does not rely on your recognition of it to be true. It is what it is.*

BELIEF

A belief is a thought you have over and over again. It shapes your perspective and is critical to Awakening because it is at the heart of what constrains you or frees you. Imagine a swirling, infinite expanse pouring Divine Intelligence into your cup, filling you with immediate and unlimited access to positive life experiences. You access this knowledge based on what you *believe*. If you believe you are your body, you live like the cup—confined by form and limited by what it can physically contain. In Reality, you are far beyond the body's limitations.

You are a subset of Divine Intelligence, whose function is to experience the world from the vantage point of your highest self. When you come to know you are always connected to Divine Intelligence, you can flow over the cup endlessly. This means you can outpace your physical limitations by accessing your nonphysical strengths. You have a sense of the *truth* of who you are. You know it as love, compassion, grace, and peace. It is more real than the material things surrounding you at this very moment. It is part of the fabric on which your very existence can be experienced. You are the movie screen, and your body simply plays out the drama of the world's story based on your thoughts.

Belief is like a valve and regulates the wisdom you allow to flow into your awareness. Limiting beliefs close the valve of Divine guidance prematurely, because your fear separates you from the truth.

As we voyage through the Universal Laws, be aware of the part of you that is greater than your physical self, like the vibrations emanating from your hands. Awareness of your fuller potential opens the valve and increases the flow of Divine Intelligence into your life. With expanded belief, you allow your cup to overflow instead being constricted by its shape. Belief is the part you play in receiving your own answers and blessings.

Your participation is not optional. It is the essential component to well-being. It is the nonform—not your physical body—that regulates how you experience life. It is what you *believe* that illuminates the Reality of life's abundance.

Awakening is an intentional effort. It is wrapped in the willingness to unlearn limitations and expectations of the body and to relearn the unlimited rewards of the larger Consciousness of which you are a part.

The biggest trick the devil ever played was convincing the world to fear failure so completely, to believe that it amputates the will, strangles courage, and blinds us all to the abundant power of the Universe. Failure is an illusion. There is no failure, only challenges to overcome on a journey of self-investigation. Change your language and change your mind. What do you believe?

Self-investigation is the critical component of this journey of transformation. It is important to question your concept of yourself because you are not who you think you are; you are much more. Ask yourself, "Who am I outside of my gender, race, familial situation, occupation, and accomplishments?" When you strip away the external titles, you allow yourself to perceive the essence of who you really are.

The awareness of your core Reality can be expanded through earnest self-exploration, stillness, or meditation. Divine Intelligence guides your thoughts to make the best choices in each moment, in harmony with all other choices occurring in the universe. As you Awaken to Consciousness, you will come to trust the unfailing nature of your True Self.

MEDITATION AND PRAYER

Prayer is a common practice in spirituality and religion, as it is the medium we use to communicate with our higher power. It is like making a telephone call to the Universe.

When you call someone, it is to directly communicate an intention or an inquiry or to experience the interaction of a particular relationship. When you pray, who are you calling and for what reason? Or do you not pray at all? If not, why? Think about the role prayer plays in your life.

Your prayers serve as wonderful evidence of your belief in a higher power. Again, we know this higher power in different ways and by different names: God, Allah, the Dao, the Buddha mind, the Universe, Source, the Great Author of All That Is, Consciousness, and so many more.

The connection frequency of prayer is reverent, still, and silent. When you pray on other frequencies, the communication signal is weak for your purposes. If you find yourself pleading to the Universe, "Why me? Are you there? Can you hear me now?" and don't hear back, then you simply need to adjust your frequency. We cover how to accomplish this in chapter on the Law of Vibration.

The most powerful prayers produce instantaneous answers—not because one person is more worthy than another, but because the *pray-er* has first prepared by ensuring an open line and clear connection to the path of communication. This path is *meditation*.

Meditation is prayer's twin. Prayer is when you talk to God, and meditation is when you listen. Generally, prayer is a call to express gratitude, give praise, or ask that forces converge to produce an outcome you desire. Meditation is the practice of stillness, going within, and attuning to the frequency that aligns you with the answers to your prayers. This is the part that most people are missing. The scripture "You have not because you ask not" is even more powerful when fortified with the Universal Laws of Awakening. *You have not because you are not on the right frequency to receive the incoming answers.* Your spiritual Wi-Fi signal is weak.

You are in the wrong frequency if your prayers have become so habitual that they have lost their meaning. You are in the wrong frequency if your prayers attempt to impress with charisma. You are in the wrong frequency if your prayers are issued as demands. The wrong frequency focuses your attention on something external to you. The Universal power is not an old man with a scepter floating in the sky somewhere, looking down on you and making chess moves with your life. Universal power, like wisdom and love, is contained in the fabric of all things, including *you*. Meditation focuses your attention to the Source of Consciousness and opens the line to receive the answers to your prayers.

Prayer is familiar, comforting, and powerful. Meditation is the single most efficacious spiritual practice for Awakening. The Universe knows what you want the instant you desire it. This makes most prayers redundant but no less powerful. An ardent prayer of "thank you" suffices, as does holding space for gratitude. The missing link for the attainment of inner peace is only *your* ability to hear the answers being provided. Receiving the answer is the blessing unto itself. Even if the answer is not the initial outcome desired, it will illuminate the wisdom and understanding that makes the desire obsolete. The Universal Laws give you the ability to receive the answers you seek.

Contemplation: Ask yourself, "Who am I? Am I attuned to receive the answers to my prayers? What do I believe?"

THE FABRIC OF BELIEF

A placebo is a pill with no active ingredients. The placebo effect is when the potency of this fake pill is as effective (or more effective in some cases) as the pill containing active ingredients. How is this possible?

Whenever you take a pill, you are *believing* it will do something. Medicine is backed by a system of trust. Whether you are aware of it or not, by taking a pill, you are trusting that it is substantiated by science and will help cure what ails you. You are believing in the doctor's education and integrity to prescribe—or the marketing that convinced you try it. So, in Reality, *belief* is the true conduit for healing and the attainment of inner peace. There are also those who do not trust healthcare or medication and believe they will have negative side effects—and then they do.

Most belief is tacit or conditioned. You believe you are going to live to see another day, even though on one unknown day you certainly will not. You believe your next breath is coming because it always has, even though it will certainly one day stop. The "I have to see it to believe it" mindset is absolutely backward and agonizingly self-limiting. Understanding your circulatory system is irrelevant to its life-sustaining performance. Understanding is not a prerequisite; however, *belief* is the real healer behind everything.

Do you think the placebo effect is somehow *fake* and medication that has active substances is *real*? Question everything you think you know about the world. The placebo effect is scientifically proven and demonstrates this truism: *when you believe in an outcome, the means to achieve it will present itself.*

The placebo effect reminds us that belief is the powerful active ingredient for all healing. Therefore, belief determines the value of your life's journey. The highest nature of your True Self is worthy of priority-one status over the body, which functions as your representative. Do not let the ego limit your true ability. Awaken to your new system of belief today—a new world is unfolding for you, and *belief* is at the core of all discovery.

Contemplation: Sit in stillness and ask yourself the essential questions, "What do I believe? What is my purpose?"

THE MIND

All change is of the mind.

This is the lesson that reverberates throughout all the Universe, consistently in all wisdom traditions. But what is the mind? It is not your brain, just as your sight is not your eyes. Your mind is nonphysical energy that emerges from Consciousness, or the One Mind. Each mind is infused with unique talents that guarantee a unique life experience. Just as your body has specific fingerprints and DNA, your mind also has a specific imprint of nonphysical characteristics. Often expressed archetypically—a hero, a leader, a caretaker, etc.—the mind contains your gifts—charisma, humor, honesty, etc.—which are the source of your perspective. If you want to change your perspective, all you must do is change your mind first.

This perspective, or your mindset, provides the context through which you perceive your experiences. If you have a mindset that there is never enough, then you will have a very different mindset about money than, say, a monk, who is also without much money but does not consider himself lacking.

Imagine you are in a dark cave with one candle. No one else is around, and you hear rain falling outside.

Does this moment spark a sense of fear or a feeling of calm? Your reaction reflects your mindset. The thoughts you create to fill in the details of the story reveal your perspective. A dark cave with a candle may sound like the perfect meditation space in nature to one person, but another may bring up images of a bear returning to that cave or rain falling so hard that it puts out the flame.

It's all in the mind.

If you are attuned to nature, you perceive solutions to your problems naturally. If you are attuned to love, you want a caring community for all. If you are attuned to fear, you may only care for yourself and your clan. The context of what you believe shapes how you experience life. Everything you perceive in life is informed by what you are attuned to, or better said, your energy or vibrational alignment.

The mind uses the brain, like sight uses the eyes, to create your framework of belief. All your attitudes, including how you feel about life itself, manifest as *thoughts* from the mind. Fortunately, you can change your mind, and therefore your life, by focusing your attention on your thoughts about what you *believe*.

The Reality is that your perception is just an opinion or a desire of the mind, which is projected as a thought and then spurs the body to action. This is how fearful thoughts cause the body to feel stress and to want to flee, even when there is no apparent life-threatening danger, and how courageous thoughts bring vitality to the body's systems.

Become an examining witness to your thoughts. Think about what you think about constantly. This introspective practice retrains your mind and brings self-awareness into every situation. Then, point your thoughts toward kindness and gratitude.

Ask yourself, "How do I want to experience the world?" Once you choose, use your *mind*. Hold each thought captive and connect with the wisdom of Divine Intelligence. The Laws of the Universe govern all minds in correspondence with the One Mind. Your thoughts and application of this spiritual operating system matter most in how you experience life.

Finally, it is helpful to know that by examining the workings of the mind, perspective, and belief, life's problems are not what they seem. The problem is *never* sex, communication, money, or the seemingly obvious. Those are knee-jerk responses of the mind, based on old, conditioned beliefs, devoid of introspection; those are responses to an unexamined mind.

While having lunch together, two women reveal their husbands are both working long hours. The first woman believes her husband is having an affair. The second woman is so proud of her husband's accomplishments at work that she never even considered he was having an affair.

When you find yourself in a challenging situation, it is a good time to practice observing your mindset. Problems bring us to the state of awareness needed for inner growth if we let them. The old, conditioned mindset perceives problems as bad, gives birth to more illusions, and obfuscates love. The first woman hates her job, and her parents divorced when she was a child due to infidelity. The second woman loves her career, and her parents are still married.

These life experiences color their perspective and satisfaction about their marriages. Their perspective about their husbands' whereabouts does not make either of their thoughts the truth.

The Universal Mindset understands that all problems are only perceived, that love exists eternally and cannot be extinguished. Enlightenment is the journey to overcoming the limited perceptions and conditioning of the mind.

Your ultimate function, then, is to remember you are an inner dimension of love, formless and limitless in potential. Hold this in your mind. *Choose* this mindset day by day because *all change is of the mind*. This is your initial step in allowing awareness to bring happiness. No plan to change the external environment will be lasting. Only this inner work will do. This is the journey of Awakening.

Contemplation: Belief is the ultimate healer in the Universe. Choose your mindset and then bring every thought to its employ. Ask yourself, "How do I want to experience the world?"

ALL IS ONE IN CONSCIOUSNESS

What is in the one is in the whole and what is in the whole is in the one.

You are like a wave in the ocean believing you are just a wave (a mind or a body). In Reality, you are the ocean (Consciousness). Your perspective is based on limiting beliefs that attach all of life's importance to the actions of the body. You know this because all your problems come from something you can hear, see, smell, touch, or taste.

Consciousness is the Reality that your spirit is part of a whole that has unlimited Divine Intelligence and capabilities vastly beyond the body's circumstance. It is this new belief system that will stifle fear and liberate you to courageously experience all life offers. The body alone cannot satisfy your infinite potential. Love, compassion, kindness, and inner peace are overflowing and are not constrained by the body.

Therefore, your primary power to create is derived from the Universe itself and conforms to the same Universal Laws as all things. *All is One.* It is your mind, not your physicality, that steers your life's direction, and it is your choices that reveal your mind's thoughts and your character. Un-Conscious thoughts perceive problems where they don't exist instead of solutions where they do exist because they are based on beliefs that are out of order with the Universal Laws.

Finally, Consciousness includes the planet and all the elements of the Universe. It is not just about human beings. Mother Earth is a living organism within the One. Expand your mind to recognize the Universal Laws evidenced in all of nature. It is this relationship that instinctively allows humankind to utilize nature's abundance to construct a modern society. We utilize math and science and believe we are masters of the Universe, forgetting that it is the Universe that provides all and that it is we who rely on it. Humankind must catch up to what Consciousness knows...

The lesson of Consciousness is that all is One, all change, and therefore creation, is of the mind, and belief and thought is its operating mechanism. As you start to unify these parts into your perception, you will see clearly what matters most.

Contemplation: Ask yourself, "Am I aware? What am I aware of? What aspect of me is aware?" The witness and awareness occur together. Become one or the other and achieve both.

UNIVERSAL LAWS OF ORDER & DESIGN

It is helpful to remember the infinite possibilities of the Universe:

1. There is a fabric of Divine Intelligence.
2. All is One.
3. The mind connects to the One through meditation and uses belief to create.

Thoughts project beliefs and reflect one's character. Unhappiness, then, is believing in an illusion instead of what is true, because joy is the resting state of Consciousness. Contentment is steeped in belief in the infinite possibilities of the Universe.

Belief that begets human kindness and compassion is the single most important force in creating a better world. History has taught us that what was once impossible—flying a plane, electricity, the internet, digital currency—is now possible. The ultimate lesson is that with belief, all things are possible. Therefore, your thoughts are the essential tools of creation.

Armed with the foundational understanding of belief and truth, you're free to delve into the Universal Laws of Order & Design. It is in mastering these laws that you will experience peace that surpasses your current understanding.

PART TWO

THE UNIVERSAL LAWS OF AWAKENING

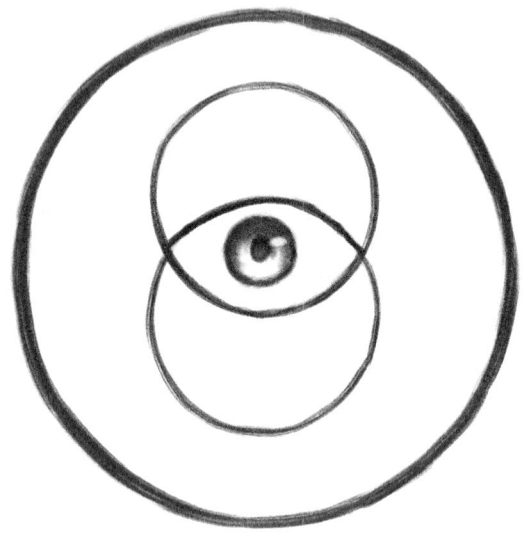

Ubuntu: I am because of you.

It speaks of the very essence of being human... Then you are generous, you are hospitable, you are friendly and caring and compassionate. You share what you have. It is to say, 'My humanity is inextricably bound up in yours.' We belong in a bundle of life.

Desmond Tutu

THE UNIVERSAL LAWS OF AWAKENING

It is usually helpful to explain the advanced concepts of Consciousness, awareness, belief, and the philosophies of the mind separately—but in Reality, they are all a cohesive *One*. Oneness is the mindset you must develop to activate the Universal Laws for your own inner transformation. This means understanding your mind is a creation or a thought of the One Mind; therefore, everything is interconnected, and everything is mental.

Look at the illustration above. The circle represents Consciousness, within which all things are contained. The space within the circle is the ethereal fabric that contains all the intelligence of the Universe. All souls are intertwined, and they are represented by intersecting circles. You are uniquely represented by the eye at the center, which focuses, believes, thinks, and perceives. You are a part of all things, and all things are a part of you. Awareness is beyond the diagram, yet it is integral to everything.

You are about to delve into the primary eleven Universal Laws of Awakening. These laws govern the operating system of the Universe. Each law is discussed singularly, yet they are all interwoven and express the same One. Use these laws for your growth or be used by them. Belief is a choice, and it is your function to chisel away at the untruths. Earnestly retrain your mind to cooperate with the Universal Laws and, from this day forward, you will experience a personal Awakening. There is a gigantic evolution in the world to bring balance to chaos. Achieving this balance requires a core shift to reorder our understanding of the Universe and change how we act and relate to one another.

People have become attached to their stories; this has become a pathology that subconsciously aims to make pain more tolerable instead of forcing us to face the discomfort of the healing process. Why do we willingly choose pain over well-being? This problem persists because we are not operating from the Universal Laws governing the All. There is One unifying force to which everything belongs. The time has come to use the Universal Laws to break this cycle of sickness.

The promise of the Universal Laws is security. The Laws of the Universe are just. They are always balanced, constant, and true. Armed with awareness of how the Universe really works, the illusion of humankind's misperceptions is revealed, and unconscious opinions and judgements naturally disappear. Every problem has a solution, and all solutions and healing are a function of Consciousness. Your true function is to Awaken to the Source within you, which is intelligent, still, eternally peaceful, and infinitely content.

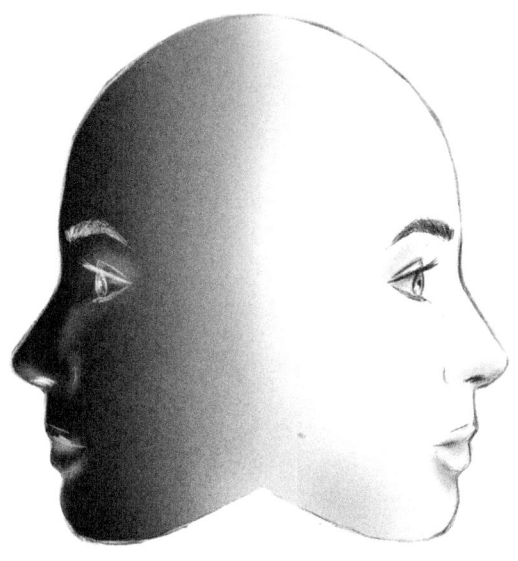

Either master your emotions or be ruled by ego.

Marquis Hunt

LAW 1: THE LAW OF LOVE & FEAR

The truth is simple. The first Universal Law strips away all complexity. There are only two emotions: *love* and *fear*. In any one moment, they cannot coexist. Therefore, you always have a choice in which lens to use. Simple.

When you are blissfully happy, by definition, you cannot simultaneously be miserable. This is because love and fear have very different vibrations and frequencies. Love builds up. Fear tears down. You can be happy one moment and sad in another moment, but you cannot be both in the *same* moment. In every instant, you can consciously choose the emotion for your best life, which is always love.

FEAR

Fear is the belief that you are your body's limitations. Fear is the darkness and the egoic lynchpin for guilt and shame. The ego is a trickster; it lures you with temptations and tricks you into believing you are deserving of them. The ego's motivator is fear. Fear scrambles truth in the mind until it makes what is true seem untrue. Fear is the belief that the body is a separate, self-regulating organism. This ideology of "separation" protects itself at all costs, including at the expense of human kindness.

Often, you recognize fear in yourself and others through judgment and competitiveness rather than compassion and creativity. This is the perspective of a separate self instead of a unified whole. Fear brings with it hate, guilt, shame, judgement, and unhappiness. It is a belief in self-preservation over the good of all. Fear, then, is the *only* reason for unhappiness. When fear is gone, joy remains.

Many ask, "How can I stop being afraid? How can I trust in others and in an ultimate good when I experience hatefulness and see death all around me?"

The answer is simple: confront your fears.

Confrontation is an antidote. When you acknowledge what you *don't* want, the Universe knows what you *do* want, and begins to reorganize and conspire for your well-being. This is an inner exploration. For example, the fear of heights is really the fear of death. Anger, jealousy, and resentment are ultimately the fear of being unworthy or undervalued. Avoid the conditioned, petty inclination to lash out and confront someone outside of yourself. Instead, look inward. This inner confrontation brings with it awareness.

Fear is a trick within the mind. It always wants the next high and is never satisfied with what already is. It is ubiquitous and always slyly encouraging you to indulge in harmful behavior. If your overall belief system is based on separation, fear will constantly emerge as the saboteur, even in happy moments.

Have you ever felt guilty about being too happy or having too much abundance? For example, a mother of two fears telling her best friend she is pregnant with her third child because her best friend has been trying to have a baby for five years. The mother is happy for her growing family yet feels guilty. This is the ego limiting access to complete joy. Compassion is the loving emotion for the best friend. Guilt is an unproductive and conditioned response. As you attune to the difference between love and fear and celebrate life more than you worry about problems, life flows more effortlessly.

Fear leads you to celebrate by overeating, drinking, and doing other things that are harmful to the body. It leads you to do the same when you are sad. In all cases, fear will never act in your best interest. Fear is choosing to believe that, no matter the odds in your favor, you will receive the worst outcome. This evolves into a lack mindset of "I am unlucky. Good things do not happen to me."

Fear can be used for Awakening, but in and of itself is not an emotion to be courted. Certainly, physical reactions to fear are helpful in times of danger to the body, but we are focusing here on the spiritual aspects of your Universal life force, which we know is infinitely more powerful.

LOVE

Love governs all the Universal Laws. So, when you don't know exactly how to release fear, simply apply any of the Universal Laws of Awakening; love will express itself naturally.

Love is the belief in the unified good, the light, and the power upholding the Universe. It is awareness, forgiveness, and peace. Love is kind and nonviolent. It is the spiritual awareness contained at the core of all things.

Love and fear appear as shadow and light in all of humankind. In every circumstance, the light of love is exponentially more powerful than the darkness of fear. Disciplined thoughts focused on loving emotions experience the power of this Universal Law quickly. The work of personal growth becomes easy because Consciousness is, in its very nature, at peace and content at all times.

Fortunately, when you are afraid, the Law of Love & Fear teaches to do just one thing: be still. For awareness brings stillness, and Awakening always chooses love.

Contemplation: "What do I want? How do I want to experience life? Is this thought based on fear? Is this action out of unconditional love?"

The lips of Wisdom are closed, except to the ears of Understanding.

The Kybalion

LAW 2: THE LAW OF ONE

Within this Law of One, all the others are contained. *What is in the One is in the whole, and what is in the whole is in the One.*

A way to understand the Universal Law of One is by envisioning circles. The line of a circle encloses a circular space, and outside the line is the atmosphere that allows the circle to be expressed. The inside of the circle, the line of the circle, and the atmosphere outside of it are all circles within circles. In Reality, whenever you perceive one circle, you are actually seeing at least three.

This Law of One is boundless. The circle is both a completion and a continuation. Imagine your life as the rings of a circle. The inside circle is your infancy, the next is your childhood, then adolescence, and so on until the final circle representing your life up to this moment. The atmosphere outside the line is your future, also known as everlasting life.

With the Law of the One, we see life's order not in time or linear events, but as it all exists *now*. You are all you have ever been and will ever be, whole and complete.

The traditional conditioned mind has difficulty thinking in the eternal now. Awareness is key to breaking this mental barrier.

THE UNIVERSAL LAWS OF AWAKENING

As the circle matures, it grows into another dimensionality, takes form, and morphs into other shapes, such as a cone, sphere, ellipse, etc. It freely explores different aspects moving inward and outward, yet always expresses its essential self: a circle. At its most infinitesimal, it is a particle of the air we breathe. At the sentient level, it is you; at the cosmic level, it is a planet; at its most magnificent, it is the Universe. The Law of One teaches that your life is just like the circle. When you can see your True Self, you are actually seeing all of creation. How magnificent is that?

As you mature, you grow into other roles—from student to teacher, or child to parent—much like the circle. You are like a tree. When a tree is cut, all the circles of its life experiences can be seen at one time. Every piece of wood shows you exactly what it is. Each ring tells you the life story of the tree—its age and the conditions it weathered every day of its life.

Just like the tree, you contain your life's story. Your past, present, and future of your spiritual life is timelessly everywhere, all at once, right now. You are well beyond the linearity of your body and can experience this limitlessness by changing your perspective. The future is a projection of the mind. Yet you exist spiritually and ever *presently* in Consciousness.

The circle contains all things within it. You are a critical and beautiful aspect in the circle of life. This is the Law of One. Essentially, you are using your body to experience life's current moment from your timeless Reality.

Contemplation: Ask yourself, "Who would I be if I had no past? What would I do if I could not fail?"

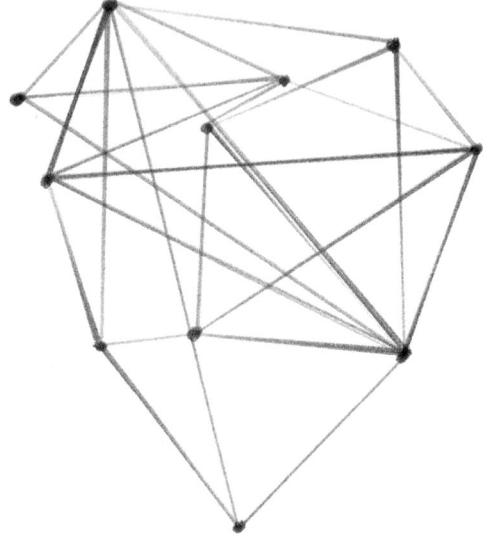

Whatever affects one directly, affects all indirectly. I can never be what I ought to be until you are what you ought to be. This is the interrelated structure of reality.

Dr. Martin Luther King Jr.

LAW 3: THE LAW OF RELATIONSHIP

People are not meant to live alone. We were created as an interconnected unit, created to be in relationship with all things. We have come to believe we are connected by the material things external to ourselves. This is true in only the tiniest sense. Yes, we need currency for transactions and food and water to live. However, the real connection, which we all realize upon broadening our minds, does not exist materially but vibrationally, in our deepest self—from the soul.

Every interaction has ripple effects throughout the Universe. The people we love and the places we live are critical parts of our makeup. Every thought you have is a unit of energy that holds the power of creation. When you have the thought to leave the house at the same time others are leaving theirs, you become part of the traffic. When you buy the last gallon of milk, you set off a chain of decision-making for the person who comes behind you in urgent need of milk. You are in relationship with everything, including your thoughts. You think about something and then it happens, down to the smallest detail.

To illustrate, become aware of your surroundings for a few moments. Everything around you first began with a thought. The building, the table, the pen, the flower, the pot, and so on. Someone thought to design, create, manufacture, distribute, grow, or cultivate every single item around you. Maybe it was you. Just as you are in relationship with these things, more importantly, you are in relationship with the thinker who had the foresight to create something you wanted and eventually found your way to.

The Law of Relationship requires a shift in perspective to the other's viewpoint. When you are hungry, the food already exists for you to eat—all you have to do is find it. The earth may provide it from your garden. Your parent, spouse, or friend may already have it for you. Perhaps it is at the restaurant, at the grocery store, or in the pantry. Whatever you need or desire comes from somewhere or someone. This is the comfort in the Law of Relationship. Everything you need already exists and can be found through your Conscious relationship to it.

In the largest sense, we come to know all our needs can eventually be taken care of because of the relationship we have with one another. In considering this perspective in all your relationships, a sense of sufficiency or even abundance arises and the urgency to figure everything out diminishes. Collectively, we are too big to fail. Your suffering does not serve the world. Help is ever present in the Universe. The Universe's grace is sufficient and realized magnificently by the Law of Relationship. Your mere existence already works in relationship with everything. Your awareness of your true existence is everything else.

You are just one star in the spectacular constellation of the whole. Yet without you, the entire connection falls apart. In Oneness, you are aware of how significant you are as a part of the whole and the power you possess. As you realize your importance and influence, you must take the relationship between your thoughts, your mind, and your beliefs much more seriously. You are a significant part of creation and of great importance. You cannot *not* matter.

Awakening to the Reality of your relationships aligns your mindset to your spirituality. Just by knowing your thoughts and intentions are intertwined within the Divine Intelligence of the Universe raises your vibration. The miracle unfolds when you understand everyone else is just as important and just as powerful as you are. You learn to grow from the power of those connections instead of shrinking away from them. Our transcendent nature is in Oneness, in relationship with others. It is not in the loneliness of selfishness. Do you feel the difference?

We cannot live for ourselves alone. Our lives are connected by a thousand invisible threads, and along these sympathetic fibers, our actions run as causes and return to us as results.

Herman Melville

COMMUNITY

Awakening shifts the collective. Instead of believing you are separate and choosing to feel powerless in life, realize every choice you face is interrelated and your life is the effect of a collective mindset. Consider your neighborhood. You are connected by the streets and the services you share. Your ideals about living are influenced by your environment and then expressed in myriad ways, from how you vote to how the streets are maintained. Is the sanitation picked up by the city, or does your community dump garbage along the roadways? What you do and how you live matters because of your relationship with your neighbors. You are in relationship by the cultural agreements of the space you share, whether you know their names or not.

In this way, each mind influences everything that happens in the scheme of the Universe. The Law of Relationship reveals itself as cause and effect from a giver and receiver. When two or more minds are aware in Consciousness, a holy trinity is created by the Law of Relationship. The clarity of combined purpose has a high Universal resonance that is a powerful attractor of beneficence and favor. If you want to start a business, it is more powerful to have collaborators, advisors, investors, customers, suppliers, etc. No success or goal can be achieved alone. This is the power of two or more.

The Law of Relationship reveals to us that, at all times, we are either being supported by or giving support to someone else. Even if you cannot visibly see or touch the evidence, trust that support is ever guaranteed by the Law of Relationship. As with all change, this trust begins in the mind. Your friendships are the easiest place to observe this law.

Once, I visited a city where I knew a lot of people. A friend's daughter contracted a serious virus and became sick and highly contagious. I had plans to stay with my friend overnight, and she would take me to the airport for my flight home.

The Law of Relationship is evident when an anonymous person exposes a young girl to a virus and the ripple effects change both her mother's plans and my plans and sets in motion my contacting other friends to get me to the airport. Meanwhile, the free time in my schedule opened the opportunity to connect with two more friends, thus altering their schedule, their children's schedule, and so on. One need only sit momentarily in Conscious contemplation to quickly see how this Law of Relationship holds everything together.

As we age, the body loses physical and mental acuity, and the mind leans strongly toward the connection of family and community. We begin to rely on others more. This simultaneously teaches the Law of Relationship while having the full experience. Governments are organized around this simple principle: take care of the collective by ensuring it can take care of itself. *The One is in the whole.*

The Law of Relationship further teaches that how you treat people has a direct impact on your life. You give so you can keep. This means I am kind so I can keep the loving emotion of kindness present in my awareness. I give to make others happy so I can keep the feeling of happiness about their good fortune in my experience. It is a wonderful law to play with because your gateway to feeling wonderful is easily accessed by making others feel wonderful. It is closely related to the Law of Giving & Receiving.

Therefore, your best and highest good is speedily attainable, in so as much as you *give* compassion to others. As we Awaken to the importance of the nonphysical aspect of relationships, rather than the material we receive in exchange, we experience joy in life.

Toxic relationships can be healed by applying this law deliberately. Let's say a couple's marriage is troubled because there is no trust. Whatever the problem, the Law of Relationship teaches that the Universe is participatory and that you have responsibility in how you experience the world. Your ownership will surprisingly help you to approach problems from a position of power and victory instead of victimhood. The key to using the Law of Relationship to heal any toxic relationship is to look at *your* relationships prior to evaluating the other person's transgression.

Relationship is the sentimental connection of a soul tethered to another. You may pass many people on the street, but when you bump into an old friend, the energy of relationship is inflamed. Recognition, excitement, and love reach a high vibration. Pass a stranger, and their presence is barely acknowledged. The Law of Relationship Awakens your connection to all things, familiar and unfamiliar, until you find the sameness that exists throughout. In this way, relationships become the mirror to the soul of the Universe.

Contemplation: Ask yourself, "Can I see the wisdom in valuing all relationships, including friends, family, strangers, and enemies alike? What is my relationship to my relationships?" Search for the essence of you that is at the core of all relationships.

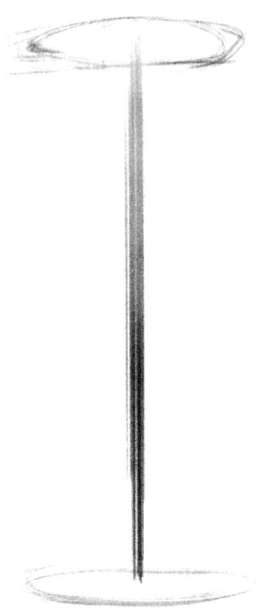

Under Heaven all can see beauty as beauty only because there is ugliness.

All can know good as good only because there is evil.

Therefore, having and not having arise together;

Difficult and easy complement each other;

Long and short contrast with each other;

High and low rest upon each other;

Voice and sound harmonize each other;

Front and back follow each other…

Tao Te Ching

LAW 4: THE LAW OF POLARITY

Armed with the understanding that all is One, it may seem paradoxical to now approach the Universal Law of Polarity (and duality). But think of it this way: a coin has two sides but is still a unified whole.

Opposites exist differently than how we commonly understand them. The Law of Polarity teaches that two sides are not in opposition; they work together in harmony to establish the whole. It is because a door is open that we can close it. It is because of death that we have life. It is because of darkness that we can understand light. Contrast broadens the spectrum of our experiences. Polarity suggests that everything is the same, only varying in degree. Your perception of opposition is a misinterpretation of Reality and is out of order with the Universal Laws of Awakening.

Take temperature, for example. At what temperature does hot become cold? This is a matter of perspective—which we know is a thought of the mind based on belief. A person who lives in the desert feels that thirty-two degrees Fahrenheit is cold, while a person in Antarctica feels that the same temperature is balmy. In the truest sense, temperature is temperature. Hot and cold, therefore, are the same—because at their root, they are both temperature.

We move along poles that are neutral and absolute. The projection of good or bad is a separation outside of the Universal Laws of One. The way we look at the world only indicates the value that we have put on what is seen, nothing more. Hot and cold are in agreement, not opposition. This is true for all things. It is only our perception that is misaligned, not the object being perceived. By using the Law of Polarity, we begin to see the perfection in everything and then make decisions from a place of sameness or Oneness, like temperature, and not from illusory perspectives, like hot and cold.

Let's take this example. A friend from a warmer region was visiting a cooler region during a chilly spring month. At home, she was used to extremely hot days year round, but here, the temperature was forty degrees colder than what she was accustomed to. Because she had checked the weather forecast, her suffering began prior to her travel with just the *thought* of the cold. When she arrived, she suffered every time she went outside, because her mind was conditioned to the experience of warmth. However, she could warm up instantly by observing her mind. Confront the cold and see what you get. It is all just weather.

It is this kind of confrontation that activates the willingness in human beings to innovate. The Law of Polarity provides this force and thus celebrates the myth of opposition. The friend focused her attention on the feeling that cold provoked in her body. She was able to become a *witness* to her mind's projections of cold instead of investing in *being* cold. Instantly, she was warmed, because awareness is nonform, unaffected by changing conditions, always content, at peace and still—and always the perfect temperature.

The Law of Polarity helps us to look beyond the fear of opposition. Imagine a pole with courage at the top and vulnerability at the bottom. At any point in life, we have infinite choices, and this pole represents your willingness to see things differently and make choices in better alignment with your purpose. The more you are willing to be vulnerable, the more you move toward courage. When you are unwilling to act upon your own best interests, the more you move toward vulnerability.

Courage is an uncomfortable feeling. It has the same base notes as vulnerability. It is a mistake to believe a courageous person is not at the same time fighting fears working to hold them back. They must be, for this is the literal definition of courage. We take the ego's version and only see glory and heroism. We say to the courageous, "Oh, it comes easily to you," without realizing that we are giving ourselves an excuse not to try.

Here is your Awakening: *it is not easy for anyone in the material*. It is always your *willingness* that moves you along the pole of transformation. Your willingness to engage on behalf of your personal story through awareness is everything. These are Universal truths: *Life is meant to be challenging. Courage is a virtue.*

The Law of Polarity teaches us to embrace the entire pole on which seeming opposites reside and acknowledge the congruency necessary for everything to exist. Those who master the Law of Polarity use vulnerability and courage *together* to defeat fear. When this law is applied, the polarized energy is brought together as an absolute, unifying force that causes fear to strangle itself and die of its own confusion. Inside of that journey, we discover the heroes, leaders, and innovators who live in each of us.

The Law of Polarity is particularly important in confronting abuse. Abuse is on one end of the pole, kindness is on the other, and each are distinctions of compassion. Abuse is a perversion of love. It is a counterattack to an attack that has only taken place in the mind. A husband beats his wife because he *believes* she threatens his authority. A wife emasculates her husband because she *believes* he should hold her in higher esteem.

Abuse is a conditioned response and is a cry for help. Become the witness and see the problem and solution as the same, because they are on the same pole. They cannot be separated, as they rely on each other to exist. This awareness causes an energetic collision of the two seemingly opposing aspects, revealing the truth of the unlimited possibilities in the Universe.

Contemplation: Ask yourself, "If there is no such thing as opposition, what do I stand for? Who determines what is good or bad? How can all things work for my good?" See the door opening the same as the door closing.

When you control a man's thinking you do not have to worry about his actions. You do not have to tell him not to stand here or go yonder. He will find his 'proper place' and will stay in it. You do not need to send him to the back door. He will go without being told. In fact, if there is no back door, he will cut one for his special benefit. His education makes it necessary.

Carter G. Woodson

REWARD AND PUNISHMENT

Humankind has been conditioned by reward and punishment. Fear has been wittingly or unwittingly introduced into "civilized" societies to create order. Ruling classes fight to maintain castes, believing a false sense of superiority can overcome an inner sense of inferiority. We are taught—and then we teach—how to evaluate everything we see through the lens of good and bad. Based on that judgement, we are then rewarded or punished. You eventually become what someone else wants you to be out of fear, instead of who you are *meant* to be. The fear of the system of punishment beats you into submission, and you are temporarily rewarded with a tiny sense of accomplishment.

Would you punish a child for not being able to walk? Degrade them for their inability to master calculus? This is what we do to one another when we presume to mandate another's development. Societally, we attach a grading system to measure achievement. "My child is so advanced, they were walking at eight months old," or "My child is slow; they didn't start walking until eighteen months" are observations distorted by the philosophy that success and intelligence are definable, that they fit inside a perfect box.

Instinctively, you know this is true, yet you blindly adopt the same system. Now, instead of being judged by others, you are the judge. You have been taught that those who rule reap the rewards and are impervious to pain. So you want to be the judge and rule and reap the rewards. But fear can only reward itself with more fear, and so the cruel cycle continues, unable to stop its own insanity. Suddenly, you have voluntarily become your own worst critic. "Why *isn't* my child walking yet?"

In the search for meaning and happiness, the question "Is this all there is?" is inevitably asked. The answer is always received through the Universal Laws of Consciousness. The conditioned mind misinterprets the answer, while the mind in alignment with Divine Intelligence receives a pristine translation. A mind in alignment exists outside of the system of reward and punishment for which we have been trained, sustained by fear. In Consciousness, the fabric of One, we experience that beauty and love are purely and wholly unaffected by the concepts of reward and punishment.

Begin to think about where you hold fearful thoughts and then locate the reward and punishment mentality that is fueling the fear. How do you break the illogical cycle of fear? There are two ways. First, you can reorient your attention toward the fear, because awareness bears reason and reason bears answers. Second, be still until a discerning moment inspires you to action. Resist all urges to make choices out of fear, worry, or regret. Meditation and introspection are where you can see the problem clearly without being led astray by the ego. A problem is still a problem. Fear is not necessary to solve it—*reason* is. And reason cannot be located when the mind is flooded with fear. With earnest striving, either of these choices will break the cycle, otherwise suffering persists.

I was afraid of being homeless. While living in one of the richest cities in the world, I witnessed homelessness every day and carried a real sense that those people living on the street were me. Early on in life, I was aware I had to make decisions that would keep this possibility a distant reality. This fear motivated me to focus on acquiring money as a reward so that I would never be punished by homelessness.

You may not see anything wrong with this perspective, but the homeless have not done anything to be punished for. Choices lead you where they lead you, but the Universe is too abundant for homelessness to continue in an enlightened society. It is a result of the cause and effect of our collective minds that allows this to continue in our lifetime. We have work to do. Reward and punishment thinking is archaic.

An Awakened person and an un-Awakened person are One in Consciousness and see the same things but perceive them differently. All things are lessons to be learned for your personal growth. Those without understanding see reward and punishment, while those with vision see love and correction. A mistake is an error to be lovingly corrected, not a sin to be punished. Missteps are integral to the natural progression of life.

When we eliminate the reward and punishment mentality, all that is left is compassion. Love is equivalent to Consciousness, just like a rose, lily, and carnation are all the same at their core; they are all flowers, yet they differ in how they express themselves. This is the same for human beings; we are different expressions of the same Consciousness.

Love and compassion are our fundamental attributes. Love has no use for performance. Love accepts what is. Fear blames and judges. You decide. Eventually, reasoning always takes over, love prevails, and balance is restored. This is where *forgiveness* dwells.

Contemplation: Ask yourself, "What am I afraid of? How do I use punishment and reward in my relationships? How can I turn a fearful thought to one of love?"

There's a season for everything and a time for every matter under the heavens:

a time for giving birth and a time for dying,
a time for planting and a time for uprooting what was planted,

a time for killing and a time for healing,
a time for tearing down and a time for building up,

a time for crying and a time for laughing,
a time for mourning and a time for dancing,

a time for throwing stones and a time for gathering stones,
a time for embracing and a time for avoiding embraces,

a time for searching and a time for losing,
a time for keeping and a time for throwing away,

a time for tearing and a time for repairing,
a time for keeping silent and a time for speaking,

a time for loving and a time for hating,
a time for war and a time for peace.

Ecclesiastes 3:1-8 (CEB)

LAW 5: THE LAW OF THE PENDULUM

The Law of the Pendulum is the swing of Universal rhythm, which is always occurring in the eternal now. Everything must change. Change has a rhythm and, ironically, is itself constant, like the changing of the seasons. The Law of the Pendulum explains the consistent, swinging heartbeat that harmonizes all things in Consciousness.

A pendulum has a bob, a string, and a fixed point and is a specific expression of change by its process of back-and-forth movement. The most critical aspect of the Law of the Pendulum in the body is breath. Your breath is connected to the breath of life, harmoniously enlivened by the nature of its constant change. It is also the connection between form and nonform, or body and spirit.

Think of the Pendulum as the undulating life force of inhalation and exhalation. As you breathe, an infinite number of interactions occur within the body. The depth of the inhale informs the powerful return swing of the exhale. One swing oxygenates the blood and powers the cells in the body to reproduce more cells. The return swing allows recovery and releases toxins and old cells back into the Universe. To the tiniest cell, this may feel like chaos, yet the rhythm is so well coordinated, the body barely notices.

The unexamined mind perceives change as unsafe, uncertain, and chaotic. For this reason, the mind views change as bad, devaluing it further by using it as an excuse to suffer. By *embracing* change, you discover security. Ultimately, that is the miracle of the Law of the Pendulum. The Law of the Pendulum guarantees constancy of rhythm, which is the changeless aspect of change. This takes us far beyond the concerns of the body and even beyond the mind, into the eternal. We know this changeless aspect as Consciousness, which is at its core pure, still, peaceful, and always content. It is also the essence of our True Self. Therefore, the Pendulum is the alchemy that turns chaos into calm.

You can use the Law of the Pendulum to solve any problem. This is achieved quickest in practicing stillness. If you have a bad day, an argument with your partner, bills you can't pay, or health issues, you are always free to go within and invoke the Law of the Pendulum. Clear your mind, then watch your thoughts as they toss back and forth in indecision. Begin to embrace the process of decision-making supported by the rhythm of the Universe. It is a natural process of calibration and an opportunity for the higher Laws of the Universe to guide every detail of life. Go within to go beyond.

The Law of the Pendulum is very useful when it comes to dealing with matters of money and, for this reason, is my favorite law. The Law of Relationship reveals humankind's frenetic attachment to money and the Law of the Pendulum brings harmony to it. Most people, whether rich or poor, feel they do not have enough money. Unexpected expenses or a job loss are common occurrences yet still send the average person into a tailspin, even when all their needs are met. Wanting more is not a problem, for the Universe is ever expanding and plentiful. It is the mindset of lack or never enough that is discordant with Reality.

Here is how to use the Law of the Pendulum. In meditation and stillness, witness your thoughts as they toss back and forth debating an issue, be it money or any perceived problem. Do so without judgment. Do not force a solution. You are not trying to solve a problem; you are *allowing* the problem to be solved by the Pendulum. Just watch and observe for a time. Your awareness is all that is needed. Calibrate your energy with the rhythm of the Universal Pendulum by witnessing your breath. Become aware of the life in each inhale and exhale and feel the focus on external problems dissipate. This will happen because peace and anxiety cannot coexist.

As you come out of stillness into activity, you will have a greater sense of calm and clarity. The Pendulum mind understands that life is not chaotic; it is *experiential*. Your function is to navigate its adventures and syncopate. The situation may still exist; however, you do not need to fret or attack, because your use of the Pendulum has assured you that in every case, all will be well. This is the virtue in patience.

The master of the Law of the Pendulum recognizes the swings in the everyday human experience and uses the rhythm to go beyond the mind's limitations. This is what it means to overcome the world. In the battleground of the world, we fight wars and compete for material things, believing that happiness and peace can be won or taken.

This is the constant lie of the ego. As you go within, the Pendulum transports you above the battlefield you are currently facing and returns to you wisdom and peace beyond your current understanding. The Law of the Pendulum harmonizes the mind with the Universal rhythm to overcome troubles. The rhythm is secure and unchanging, a constant friend in times of need.

We fall short of our full potential because of two things. First, impatience for the Pendulum to swing back into one's comfort zone causes the mind to be out of rhythm and wreaks havoc. The second reason is simply a lack of awareness. With awareness, we are able to join in the rhythm of the Pendulum in peace, never in fear.

The Law of the Pendulum awakens us to the subtle and constant beginnings and endings at play in a never-ending Universe, reminding us that change is life-affirming. Change confirms that what we do *matters* and that redemption, forgiveness, and a brighter day are always promised. I suggest you start with this law and come back to it over and over again for peace and restoration.

Contemplation: Ask yourself, "Are there any problems that cannot be solved?" Throughout the day, stop and take three breaths to consciously sync with the Universal rhythm.

Everything in Life is Vibration.

When something vibrates, the electrons of the entire universe resonate with it. Everything is connected. The greatest tragedy of human existence is the illusion of separateness.

Albert Einstein

LAW 6: THE LAW OF VIBRATION

Everything vibrates. Everything from a rock to a thought resonates with vibration at varying frequencies. Fundamentally, everything is energy, and this energy has resonance throughout the Universe. This is the Universal Law of Vibration. The highest vibrations do not have form, like sound waves and sunlight. Love, compassion, and kindness have the highest vibrations in the Universe.

Lower vibrations have density and therefore a weightiness that exists in material or things with form—from plants to people. However, the formless features of fear and hate also have low vibrations. It helps to think of vibration as the bridge of all communications in the physical and nonphysical, or the spiritual. Spiritual vibration is not objectively measured by a yardstick or in megahertz; it is evidenced by awareness and emotion in each moment. High-vibration energy feels like sunny days, happy people, laughter, and creativity. Low-vibration energy feels like gloom, anger, and apathy.

Vibration conducts things we cannot see with the naked eye. Imagine a tornado and its movement of air. We call it wind at first, and then a tornado or storm when it moves forcefully. What is it that makes air turn into wind? What power or confluence of events forces the seas to rage and the clouds to open? It is all by the power of vibration. Vibration creates. Personal growth comes from the awareness of the vibration in all things, because *this* you can manage.

Take a moment to experience the essence of life through the lens of vibration. Imagine a big family dinner around a table. What energy do you feel? Is it love? Or is it about the hassle of the travel that brought you to the table? Your awareness of your emotions helps reveal your vibration in each moment.

The Law of Vibration leads you to your Inner Self. To achieve any and all states of being, you can raise or lower your vibration to the energetic match of that which you desire. First, focus your attention on higher vibration feelings. The quickest way to do this is to do something kind for someone else.

Raise your vibration daily by being in nature, around high-vibration people, and around anything that leads you into peacefulness. Conversely, you can remove yourself from people and circumstances that drain your energy.

Peace, stillness, and silence are high-vibration aspects of awareness. All the desired outcomes match the level of vibration they hold. As we Awaken to our personal energy and the energy of the planet, we begin to understand vibration as the language of the Universe and can use it to choose and communicate for the good of all things.

Let's take the following as an example. A senior leadership team was sitting around a huge boardroom table, waiting for the president of the company to enter. It was the end of the year. No one was meeting their targets; public perception was bad; and everyone was certain a good, old-fashioned tongue-lashing was about to ensue. The vice president entered the room first and felt the tension. Everyone was quiet. No one made eye contact. The vibration was palpable, filled with anticipation and fear. The vice president felt—and almost joined her colleagues in—the vibration of fear. She stopped and took a conscious breath, aware that a difficult meeting was imminent. Then she chose to raise the vibration of the room. So, she looked around the room, smiled at everyone, and said, "Breathe."

A collective sigh of relief and nervous laughter were released, and the vibration of the room was immediately lifted. The higher vibration indicated a level of support and understanding that was being distorted by the sense of fear. A more balanced and honest exchange was better for the company, better for the people, better for the world.

Use awareness to raise the vibration in all situations in your life to get to what matters most—the meaning behind the answers. Fearful responses are rife with spin and conjecture, signifying nothing. Your highest energy creates the best version of yourself.

Remember, every thought matters, as they are a unit of energy that connects us in relationship to one another. Close proximity to low vibrations brings you down. This is why awareness is key. When you become aware that you are out of sync with your desires, do this: stop, breathe into your inner being, and access the higher vibrations of Divine Intelligence in stillness.

As you Awaken to the aspects of Consciousness, your vibration stays elevated longer. Eventually, your resting vibration becomes resilient to the ups and downs of life. You create a point of attraction that is high enough to raise the energy around you (instead of being whipped around by others' thoughts).

It is a miraculous stage of Awakening when you discover how to use the Law of Vibration to attract better feelings and outcomes. The secret is simply *choice*. If you feel stuck in a low-vibration mode of depression or guilt, simply do this awareness exercise to get unstuck and improve your energy.

First, it is important to be honest and admit to your Inner Self how you feel. Take fifteen minutes to release your anxieties into the Universe. A ritual of writing down your woes and then burning or burying them is a very cleansing and satisfying start. Confront the feeling that you want to go away. Then, spend another fifteen minutes answering the questions in the following contemplation.

Contemplation: Ask yourself, "What qualities would I need to develop to let my Highest Self emerge? Am I using wisdom in all my interactions? Am I aware of my power?"

*If you want others to be happy, practice compassion.
If you want to be happy, practice compassion.*

Dalai Lama XIV

LAW 7: THE LAW OF GIVING & RECEIVING

Is it better to give than to receive? As we reorder our understanding of the world using the Universal Laws, we learn giving and receiving happen in unison, not one after the other. Cause and effect always occur at the same time. Inhaling and exhaling exist together. By separating the concepts in your mind, the transmission loop is lost. Giving and receiving opens the flow of blessings through the vibration of *gratitude*.

The Law of Giving & Receiving teaches us that you get what you give. Therefore, you instantly receive the blessing yourself by blessing others. It happens through energy and vibration. It is not the material gift that matters most; it is thought that gives way to giving, and it is thought that leads the way to receiving. You are more than your body and materiality. Everything is mental.

Consider the parent-child relationship. You raise your child in love and, in turn, feel loved—learning as you teach and teaching while you learn. Even something as small as appreciating the clean smell of the newborn baby makes you marvel in wonder at all of life. Gratitude and blessings work in the same way. As a child, love and trust are a natural state of being—but then the fears and judgements of the world inspire the opposite. Again, there are no opposites, only variations among a spectrum of Oneness—and because the Universe is kind, here you are again.

As you give gratitude, you receive blessings; as you are blessed, you are grateful. It is the circle of life, and it is the Law of Giving & Receiving. You are never depleted by giving. You give so you can receive. The ego twists this spiritual law and tries to apply it to the material, but it doesn't work that way in spirituality. Here we are referring to unconditional giving. You don't give to others so you can keep an investment or tax write-off that demands a return. The power of giving is in the nonform dimension. It feels like encouragement or being supportive. The meaning behind the gift is what matters most, and the tax credit is a byproduct.

The Law of Giving & Receiving teaches that gratitude paves the way for receiving the sort of blessings you will be even more grateful for. It teaches that when you give to someone in Consciousness, you also give to yourself. Gratitude completes of the cycle in the same instant.

The demands of society are insatiable, whereas the Universe demands nothing. A people pleaser undervalues themself by believing other people's opinions over their own truth. This leaves no room to receive. An entitled person constantly expects to be rewarded, which leaves little room for giving. The Law of Giving & Receiving teaches to give in the energy of gratitude *while* you recognize the vibration of gratitude within you.

To give begrudgingly is not a gift—it is actually *a taking*. It takes away joy, which lowers one's vibration to a frequency that is too low to receive the blessings of giving. When you give with gratitude, you receive gratitude immediately. Gratitude has these two points of entry but is still only the one thing. Giving is the access point of receiving. It has nothing to do with the gift itself.

When you feel unappreciated after giving up your time, money, or talent, it is because the intent of your giving was really to make yourself feel better. A true gift is from the spirit. Expecting some sense of gratitude and excitement as reward for your giving removes the gift part of the exchange. The sign of infinity expresses this never-ending flow of life always giving back to itself, maintaining the balance and harmony of the One.

Imagine a pothole in the street outside your home. Now, imagine you wake up tomorrow and the pothole is a crater as wide and deep as the Atlantic Ocean. It is difficult to fathom. Our human ability to conceive the vastness of the Universe is extremely limited. Infinity is not *many* things—it is the *One* common thing. It is the answer in which all equations converge. It is *Consciousness*, of which we are a critical part.

Contemplation: Ask yourself, "Do I require a return on my giving? Is this generosity? Do I receive freely?"

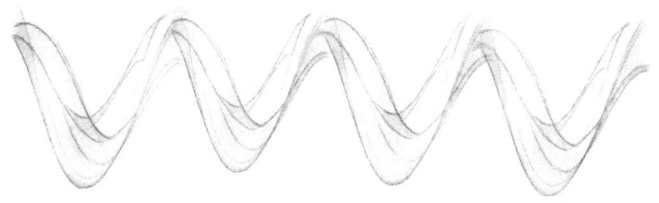

In this world you will always have trouble. But Take heart! I have overcome the world.

John 16:33 (NIV)

LAW 8: THE LAW OF EBB & FLOW

Everything in life ebbs and flows. There will always be peaks and valleys. This answers the age-old questions, "Why did this happen to me? Why do bad things happen to good people?" Take comfort in that what happens to you in life is not personal—it is simply a result of the vibration of your thoughts attracting that which you focus on. Everything is connected and interacts through cause and effect.

We know enough of the Universal Laws by this point to see the power of mindset. Good and bad are definitions of the ego; the two emotions that frame your life are fear and love; all change occurs by the Law of Vibration; everything happens in Consciousness and in connection to all other things; nothing happens to you alone because what is in the One is in the whole.

The belief that bad things shouldn't happen to good people is flawed, because there are not inherently *good* or *bad* things. Every experience in life holds value, even and especially the experiences most of us consider to be negative or uncomfortable. Most of our personal growth can't be credited to an easy, privileged, effortless life. In most cases, that credit goes to "negative" experiences in which we've had to change for the better to progress. It is more comforting to believe that good things should only happen to good people, because then you are given a false sense of control over how you think the world should be by assigning what you believe is good and what you believe is bad.

It has been emphasized that Reality exists irrespective of your opinions of it and that your beliefs manifest at the level of vibration that you exude. Universal Laws are always in effect, and you get what you ask for as much as your awareness allows you to receive.

For instance, a person dislikes their job situation and begins to turn assignments in late and to sabotage their boss with bad information. The Law of Ebb & Flow guarantees that this person will eventually find other employment or a new boss, because times of trouble are followed by times of contentment. However, actions and thoughts based in fear and will attract other low-vibration outcomes. This person may find another job but will remain unhappy until their vibration changes.

The Law of Ebb & Flow teaches awareness of this Universal rhythm to encourage your higher vibration of hope and anticipation as a reminder that all things are working for your good. Instead of focusing on sabotage and emotions of resentment, a higher vibration focuses on pursuing new opportunities, which yields quicker results that support one's purpose. When your beliefs align with what the Great Author of All That Is has ordered by the Universal Laws, your life experiences become blissful.

Universal Laws can't be changed or broken. Man-made laws, yes; Universal Laws, no. The Law of Ebb & Flow demonstrates the Universal kindness and inclusion of all Universal Laws within each Universal Law. Positive and negative exist in vibration, in polarity, and can be found as the basis for all things. They are neither good nor bad, as the ego would judge. Consciousness doesn't judge, cheat, punish, or reward. It has no need to, because everything starts and ends within it. Bliss and peace are the screen on which ebb and flow resonate.

Remember, the purpose of life is to be an expression of Consciousness or Divine Intelligence, experiencing all things in which both peaks and valleys play an active role. Don't we all want to experience both the ebb and the flow, like the dance of the moon and the sun? This is the nature of growth and the rhythm of the Universe. It is law.

According to *Webster's*, the definition of *fair* is "marked by impartiality and honesty: free from self-interest, prejudice, or favoritism."

The world is not "fair" because, collectively, we lack awareness. Still, it is our function to bring fairness into the world because *all things are One*. As you recognize ebb and flow in your life, you come to understand that even in the valley, when the tide ebbs, you are not guilty of your circumstance. You cannot be a failure because in each moment you are still becoming. The tide will flow after it ebbs. A low point is not a failure because it is not an ending. You belong to, and are integral to, all things, and you are experiencing life the way it is designed—with peaks, valleys, ebbs, flows, all of it. Shame and worry are energy kidnapped by the ego to keep you blind to how essential you really are. Let these aspects go.

THE UNIVERSAL LAWS OF AWAKENING

The Law of Ebb & Flow teaches that your very experiences are an essential thread in the fabric of life. Therefore, in the highest sense, consider it pure joy when troubles of any kind come into your life. In Reality, they are wake-up calls to remind you of your significance; reminders to use your power to continue to grow. This is where you use your vulnerability to activate courage, simultaneously raising the vibration of the world. Invite the risk and accept what is. This is the work that must be done first for your power to emanate.

Because everything is in relationship, you cannot know joy without pain. Without contrasts, everything is the same. The world is designed to have both joy and pain. If you think you should be excused from pain, you must accept you will also be devoid of pleasure. The Universal Law of Ebb & Flow assures that you will always rise from the valley. It is also true that you must embrace the fact that to rise from a valley, you must first fall from a peak.

A master of the Law of Ebb & Flow no longer characterizes everything as good or bad as the world perceives it. As you Awaken, you come to embrace every experience as one from which to grow. You understand that *all life events and experiences are simply lessons to be learned.*

Think about where you are wounded and the circumstances that cause you pain. The Universal Laws create a happy life without any consideration for the accumulation of stuff. Stop thinking about what you want materially as more important or vital than the Laws of the Universe. Miraculously, this shift makes attaining what you want easier.

Problems are not punishments from the Universe. They are the events specifically tailored to promote your spiritual growth. Avoidance stunts you. Today, you learn that you are fine the way you are, because problems come and go in the natural ebb and flow of things. You did what you were taught, but you were simply given the wrong direction. However, Awakening to your happiness requires you to boldly practice the Universal Laws and allow your growth and spiritual Awakening to happen naturally. Let go of the past and accept that everything ebbs and flows. *Everything.* It can be no other way.

Contemplation: Ask yourself, "What does it feel like to be complete. How can I turn impatience into anticipation?"

To see a World in a Grain of Sand
And a Heaven in a Wildflower
Hold Infinity in the palm of your hand
And Eternity in an hour...

William Blake, "Auguries of Innocence"

LAW 9: THE LAW OF SILENCE

In the famous "Flower Sermon," the Buddha silently holds up a single flower to the assembly of his disciples. After a time, the follower Mahākāśyapa smiles, indicating his understanding. The lesson is that true wisdom needs no words. The Law of Silence reminds us of the place where all minds are joined in wisdom and stillness, the place that is the life force of all there is.

If you look for wisdom and knowledge, you will not find them with what your human senses can see, hear, touch, taste, or smell. The wrong lens cannot correct vision. Can you bake a cake with a hammer? Or build a stable house with salt? The transmission of wisdom is a unique expression not translatable by the sensorium. If you can only get wisdom and guidance from complete sentences or can only see miracles with your eyes, you miss the point. Wisdom is in the *awareness* of experience.

Why are metaphors, art, music, and creativity so beautiful? They expand upon the spoken word with nonform, through rhythm and a vibration that connects directly to happiness and joy. Words are not necessary. Art appreciation is silent awareness and a direct connection with a beauty and understanding that words cannot adequately convey.

Eyes do not create sight and ears do not create sound. The body is a tool that translates energy and vibration into senses, which are useful for basic human interactions. These physical senses harmonize into experiences. The body is like a piano, an instrument translating vibration into sound with each keystroke. Keys played together harmonize and create new sounds that are arranged into song. Your body is the piano, you are the song, and your life is a symphony. Life is endlessly creative, continuously swirling in a cycle of striving and attaining. This is what we call *harmony*.

The brain does not house or create thoughts. The *mind* does. The brain's function is to translate thoughts from the mind to be used by the body. The body's function is to carry out the communication it receives from the brain. The body represents life through its experiences, yet it is not life itself.

Spend time in nature, observing art, seeing the patterns, the geometry, and the beauty. Observe how a flower is silent, rests in peace, yet still grows, breathes, plants roots into the ground, and lifts its face toward the sun. Nature teaches us the Universal Laws by expressing all the Universe is without perceptible words or motion. In this miraculous way, the planet speaks to us and moves us more deeply, and as we Awaken, we experience this as grace.

There is a silence underneath all things, in between each word and underneath all action. It is what you are made of—Consciousness. Find this essence of yourself. Spend time there.

Contemplation: Ask yourself, "Who was I before I was born? Who am I talking to when I talk to myself? Where is the place beyond my mind that is completely quiet?" Go there repeatedly until you can stay for a while.

I am under no law but God's.

Lesson 76, *A Course in Miracles*

LAW 10: THE LAW OF DIMENSIONALITY

An illusion is something that is wrongly perceived or understood by the senses. For example, time is an illusion. It is not what you think it is, and it is much more than magic tricks or sleight of hand. Your Awakened mind is beginning to understand that illusions are the basis for how we are taught to experience life as a collective—*your opinion versus mine*. Each person perceives life differently, and in this way, everything is an illusion to someone else. This means that reality as we know it is itself an illusion—or rather a compilation of collective illusions.

You have learned that *time* is a linear expression of past, present, and future, and this was substantiated by Isaac Newton's laws of motion. However, years later, Albert Einstein proved that time is actually *relative*. Your *experience* of time depends upon the conditions of the moment. Your perception of time is a generalized agreement as it pertains to movement and location. For example, I get to work at 8:00 a.m. There is an agreement about what 8:00 a.m. means, including the time zone, so everyone can arrive at the correct time. This agreement of time allows me to harmonize my interactions. I therefore calibrate to wake up at 6:30 a.m., meet friends for lunch at noon, and so on.

Remember, regardless of whether you agree with the order of things, Reality is Reality, and it exists with or without your understanding. The linear concept we grew up with has been proven false, as Einstein proved that time bends and contracts relative to space and energy. If you believe past, present, and future are linear movements, you are living in an *illusion* of time. Scientists and spiritualists alike agree on this. Now is the time to update mistaken perspectives about the world.

Time is relative. You have been trained to live as if time is absolute. The faster the movement, the more space contracts and time appears to slow down. If I take a jet to travel three thousand miles, I'll arrive at my destination in five hours. But if I drive the same distance, it will take fifty hours. If I walk that distance, it will take much more *time*.

Time and movement are in relationship, but only movement, or *vibration*, is a Universal Law. Everything vibrates, and so time moves in relationship with our true selves, not the reverse. Said differently, time is a byproduct of dimensionality used by the five senses to harmonize physical interactions in the world. The Law of Dimensionality teaches us that we are not the servants of time and are not twisted into its constraints; we are the *masters* of it. Spiritual or nonform interactions are out of time. They are timeless or what we call eternal.

Space is another variable in the illusion of time, but again, energy is constant. Consciousness expresses itself through energetic vibration. Time *appears* as waves of energy moving faster or slower within space. These vibrations create frequencies that express themselves as colors of light and variations in density. This energy sets the conditions for matter and physical worlds to exist. Flowers bloom and people are born. The gestation period for growth is only measured by time. Time and space are conditioned to each other so completely that they too are One thing.

In all the Universe, physical planets have the conditions for matter and space to be created, expressed through time. It is a measurement. Stop giving time a life of its own. "There's not enough time" or "I had a great time" are common expressions that reinforce the illusion, and not the Reality, of time.

Time by itself is neither good nor bad. We have nothing but time. How you value it is a matter of perspective, not the unchangeable truth of Reality. Time does not happen to you or pass you by. You create the vibration at which you operate by choosing *how* you operate, which then affects how you experience the relative aspects of time and space.

The higher your vibration, the closer you are to awareness of Consciousness and Source energy. The high-energy vibrations produce more power, and desired results are produced quicker, like a jet travel vs snail travel. This is the Reality of what we call time. Time *does* fly when you're having fun, and it *does* move slowly when you are bored or in a lower vibration. Your perception of time moving quickly or slowly is not the illusion, it is the truth. You *do* have the ability to speed or slow time based on your energy modulation, because doing so happens within. You do it all the time, unconsciously.

In Awakening, you begin to use past information to handle the present and influence the future. You realize everything happens at the same moment, not linearly. A memory is a thought occurring in the present moment. There is no past until you think about it in the now. When you react to the past, you are projecting your thoughts about the past into the present moment. You give the concept of the past the power over your current circumstances.

Consciously create the future in the present moment by using the Law of Dimensionality. Your awareness changes your vibration and slows down or speeds up the results manifested in the material realm. If I want to lose weight, then in each present moment, I must be conscious of what I eat and how active I am in order to create the future body of my imagination. A future weight is reliant upon what I do in the present moment. The future is nothing. I create today. I experience now. The future is a thought, an abstract potential—and without awareness, it is barely a wish.

Think about a rocket and a snail. A rocket uses a high level of physical vibration (energy) to shorten the time of travel. While a snail moves so slowly when crossing the road that it seems to take forever. And so, it does. Low energy is slow and dense, lengthens the perception of time, and makes time seem to go by slowly.

Initially this understanding of the Law of Dimensionality will significantly help you to change your view of the world by changing your perception of time from slow and fast to short and long. Ultimately, even this perception will vanish as you Awaken and live in each moment knowing that time is neither here nor there—it is eternal.

What you think of as time can be also understood differently as the space between the present moment and its manifestation. Time is energy and space; it is not the hands of a clock. Like the body, time measured by a clock or a calendar is a tool for the collective Consciousness to communicate in the material world.

In truth, life is in such constant movement that even the present moment has already passed by the time you realize it. We think of the speed of light as instantaneous, yet it takes eight minutes for the light of the sun to reach the earth. In this way, by the time we see something with our eyes, it has already existed in what we know as the past, no matter how short the timeline. Our body can never catch up to the Reality of any instant, but our True Self is always present in Consciousness. In awareness, we are light-years ahead of the planet.

You have been told before, probably in many ways, that you are not your body, that you are so much more. You must know this understanding is fundamental to living a life of joy because it refocuses your awareness to what is of primary importance: your mind. The body is a translator of energy so that we can communicate with one another in form. The spiritual dimension from which the body operates is more powerful, as it is interconnected in Consciousness. It is the *I Am*.

The truth about the soul is that it exists outside of time and space, and therefore cannot be *limited* by time nor space. The soul is limit-less. Where the soul exists is pure Consciousness—a space of stillness, an ever-present sea of the known and unknown flowing together and wrapped around one another so symbiotically, they cannot exist separately. What seems like emptiness is actually the fullness of being in Conscious alignment with the One. What looks like darkness is overcome by light. Silence is the language of God—still and empty. Yet it is here where we find our purpose, which is primarily spirit and instructs the right actions for peace for all humanity.

Now is not just a moment in time, it is *all* that ever is. It is the eternal now in which all experiences happen. Consciousness rests in the now, in the I Am.

Contemplation: Ask yourself, "What would I do if I could not remember the past? What would I do if I knew I could not fail? Why fear the future?"

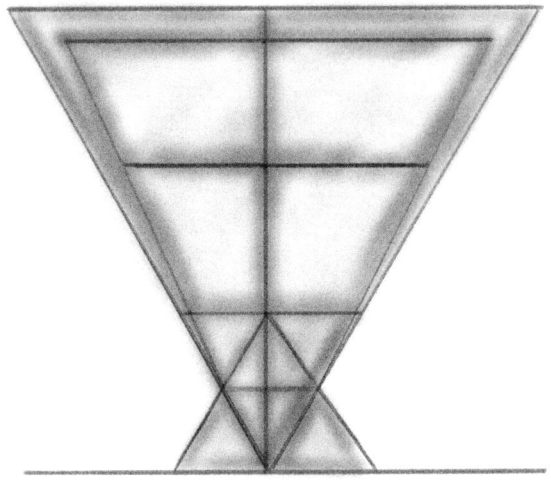

What is necessary to change a person is to change his awareness of himself.

Abraham Maslow

LAW 11: THE LAW OF SELF-ACTUALIZATION

Maslow's hierarchy of needs uses a pyramid to reflect and prioritize the basic needs of human survival. The very bottom represents our most basic physiological needs—food, water, shelter, rest, etc.—whereas the sliver at the top represents one's need for self-actualization. Because we are much more than our body or physical form, this thinking limits our ability to solve the mundane problems of the world with Divine Intelligence. Here is where we infuse our knowledge of the Divine fabric and its limitless potential into our daily thoughts and regimens.

Let's go back to the bottom of the pyramid—the part that represents the body's traditionally accepted hierarchy of needs. Maslow posits that food, water, shelter, rest, and the other basic needs must be met before one can be motivated by the needs reflected at the top of the pyramid—purpose, fulfillment of potential.

As we become aware of Consciousness and the Universal Laws, we understand that self-actualization is not something you work on after you figure out what to eat, where to live, and what to wear. Knowing oneself is at the center of being, which then opens the way to fulfilling all other needs. Self-actualization is not something that happens at the top of a pyramid, once you have met all the other needs of the body; it is the pole that runs through all things and that binds and strengthens all of life's needs at once. It is as crucial to life as a load-bearing support beam is to a building. It is not a process to be achieved but rather the *isness* through which achievement happens. The Law of Self-Actualization teaches that food and shelter are in service to your life, not the other way around.

This means knowing your true nature is the foundation for happiness. Even if you have a feast every night for dinner, wear the latest fashions, own a big house, and have a reliable career, suffering will always be your focal point until awareness self-actualizes. If you think of yourself as *only* a body, you will never have enough because the ego is insatiable. The same stressors will simply show up in a different skin. It will look like frustration with overextended time commitments, body-shaming, or a need to keep up appearances to meet the expectation of others.

The self-actualized part of you is always content because you come to know yourself as an essential part of a whole. Your Awakening reminds you that you cannot fail, all things are working for your good, and perspectives are simply a reflection of upbringing and can be changed. In Awakening, you find what you never lost—the confidence that life always provides. Then the spiritual nature of prosperity is revealed and can be enjoyed without hesitation.

Is a hungry person unhappier than one with a full belly? Hunger is of the body, and happiness is of the spirit, and they are not on the same polarity or vibration. Use the

Universal Laws to Awaken and separate the apples from the oranges. Tear apart these old notions in your mind.

While it is true that we require food to live, it is hunger that finds food, the same way thirst finds water. The Universe always provides. By yourself, you accomplish nothing. This is how life works. Consider that every day when you leave the house, you do not know where each sip of water or bite of food will come from. You do not know where you will need to relieve yourself, but you trust there will be a toilet or, if it comes down to it, a bush. Your awareness of all relationships helps to bring accomplishment. This self-actualization is at the center of who you are. Self-actualization is Awakening. This is when you begin to flow with life.

Invariably, a person who struggles to see themselves as a soul instead of just a body will ask the question, "What about those who die of hunger? They can't be expected to concern themselves with Consciousness and spiritual matters when starving!" This is exactly what is expected for resolution. The ego assumes a level of suffering, which it projects onto others, and keeps hunger instead of supply in its vibration.

A person who fasts for weeks is hungry yet glorified by the earnestness of their journey. A person who hungers because of the unkindness of humanity can also come to self-actualization *because* of their arduous circumstances. How much more earnestly do you pray when suffering than when not?

Beautifully, a self-actualized person is a force for change because, through their awareness, they give freely and thus receive the blessings of wisdom. Just like one flame can light many candles, an enlightened person brings more light into the world by *sharing*. You cannot be depleted by sharing. You never lose by giving. Often, people who have been impoverished are more willing to share what little they have than the unactualized wealthy because they know the gratitude of receiving and therefore the graciousness of giving. This is where compassion explodes into the miraculous.

The unactualized wealthy person does not share or give without wanting something in exchange. They believe an exchange is only worth making if there is a certain return on investment they can anticipate. But what is kindness? Kindness is not an exchange. It is a gift. A fair exchange is simply a fair exchange.

You have not necessarily done anything kind when you pay for a service at market price, at discount, or when you lavishly overpay. Kindness is nonphysical. Carefully examine when you are giving freely from a place of self-actualization for the Universal good or when you may be unwittingly exploiting the world. Kindness is the thought behind the gift and may or may not cost money.

For example, a person employs a homeless person and then an illegal immigrant to clean their house and feels that the workers should be overly grateful. Is it a favor to pay another human for the value received from their service? What do socioeconomic status or immigration status have to do with *your* equity, compassion, or Oneness? In Reality, nothing. Self-actualization brings clarity to why you do what you do and to the essential question, "Who *are* you?"

The elite congratulate themselves thinking they are separate from or better than being part of the One that connects all things. Distrustful due to their own beliefs, they think others should elevate themselves, not realizing they too have been lifted by the kindness of others. It is entitlement that destroys. Transcendence occurs when we come to realize it is compassion that builds and makes the world a better place.

As you self-actualize your life possibilities, you too unfold exponentially by the Law of Relationship. The unfolding happens quickly because of the high-vibration energy, and time lengthens or shortens in your favor. You see your life as multifaceted, a well-rounded sphere of life, and all things are made clear. This is self-actualization. It too contains and is contained by all the Universal Laws.

Everyone Awakens or self-actualizes eventually, even if it happens with their last breath. Don't wait. Know thyself. The time is now.

Contemplation: Ask yourself, "Who am I? What do I want? What is my purpose?"

PART THREE

THE BODY AND THE WORLD

For though we walk in the flesh, we are not waging war according to the flesh. For the weapons of our warfare are not of the flesh, but have divine power to destroy strongholds.

2 Corinthians 10:3-5 (ESV)

THE BODY AND THE WORLD

Spirit wanted to experience itself in discrete ways. Feminine and masculine, tall and short, black and white, able-bodied and disabled, and so on. All at once, it brought forth all scenarios in interplay, creating infinite potentiality. First, the Universe, the galaxies, the stars, and the planets. Then came their elements—fire, air, water, and wind. After that was the emergence of bacteria and germs, evolving eventually into plants and animals. And then, of course, there is *you*. Humankind.

Somewhere along the way, you forgot that you are a spiritual being having a physical experience, that your body's sole function is to let the spiritual characteristic emerge through you to glorify and satisfy the whole. Life is then the spiritual interaction of all experiences coexisting, from the rotation of galaxies to the rhythm of your breath. And so, all things are born of One Universal intention, functioning according to the Universal Laws, in tandem with creation itself.

You might believe that the experiences of your body are more important than the experiences born of your spirit.

You keep your thoughts where you feel you have control, and you believe your well-being to be more important than the whole. You care only about what the world can do for you. Unfortunately, the Universe does not operate in this belief system.

You have no doubt heard a version of the creation story in your spiritual or religious traditions. It is true that you are born from nothing, given a body to be a unique expression, and will return to the vastness of Consciousness.

The Universal Laws of Awakening describe the design and order of all things and underscore the Universal wisdom that you are not your body. It is not your own. It was paid for with a price. Turn your attention to your True Self, which is the effusive energy of spirit that interconnects with everything else. Armed with the Universal Laws, you are weaponized to operate at a higher frequency in the world. You can Awaken and take back your power (which is always there) and stop being used by the world for illusory desires and illogical outcomes.

By consciously using your mind and body together for the attainment of inner peace, you instantly become a warrior of good and love *for* good and love.

THE BODY

Your body is an amazing instrument, but it is just that—an instrument. It is not who you are. Your body is merely your representative. From your first breath to the ever-present eternal now, notice how the body changes. It grows in weight, height, and features, and the mind changes from processing infantile to mature thoughts. Now, take your attention to your Inner Self, the most critical aspect of yourself. It is neither male nor female, it is impervious to hot and cold, and it is untouched by external physical conditions. This is the part you that is aways present, whether experiencing pain or joy, whether awake or asleep. This is the Consciousness through which change occurs yet is itself complete and never changing. This aspect of you is the most critical to inner peace and happiness, more so than the body.

As we age, we experience a type of vertigo where we know we are getting older but we still feel youthful. Suddenly, we cannot reconcile chronological age with the true nature of the soul. This is because of the *false belief* that as the body ages, the essential Self must also be changing. It does not. It matures, but it does not age. As you Awaken to Reality, you become confused by the false belief that you are your body.

Recognize that the *I Am-ness* of your true nature does not change with time. As we mature, we Awaken to the vibrations of our bodies in relationship to the world. We begin to attune to nature—like the ticking of a clock, the hissing of steam—and follow the melody as it disappears into its last note. We come to understand that life is beyond skin and bones. These vibrations are the energy source of life that powers the body. It is the connection to the All. To identify yourself with only your body is to severely misunderstand the nature of your vast Self and to usurp your own natural ability to activate the essential power within you.

You exist prior to your body's incarnation, and the vibrational aspect of yourself continues long after your body decays. This is what it means to have *everlasting life*. You know this instinctively and are surely aware of the concept if you participate in any religion. This is *heaven here on earth.* The human error is believing you have to wait to have everlasting peace until after the body has transitioned. This is not true. You have everything you need already within you. It is of Consciousness—pure awareness and wanting of nothing. The essential nature in Consciousness never changes.

Your body does not contain your spirit. Your body is contained *within* your spirit. Here is how you know this is true. When you talk to yourself, who are you speaking to? Your body? Is it you that sees the table, experiences the wind, and walks on two legs? If you cannot see with your eyes or walk with your legs, or if you fall into a coma and cannot communicate with your mouth, the essential part of you still exists. Investigate this part of you. Knowing what you are *not* is the way to discover what you *are*—and you are *not* your body.

Your body is a compilation of movement based on the *Universal code*. The code of Consciousness creates energy centers throughout the body. This is the process of Consciousness modulating itself into matter. We gain the experience of sensation, touch, intuition, feeling, and thought from this primordial energy. It is these energy centers that hold the body together and power its operation. These vortices are widely known as chakras. The body is within the vortices, which hold it together. Your body is enlivened as a result of these energies working together harmoniously. When these energies are blocked or misaligned, sickness occurs. Understand that your body is a direct reflection of your spiritual health. Your spirit is the first essential part of you.

THE WORLD

The Fibonacci sequence and the golden ratio reveal that a code exists within Consciousness, which reveals itself over and over again in the fabric of life. These patterns of code produce shapes as well as vibrations. The simultaneous spinning, rotating, and undulating creates first a harmony and then a physical form.

There are elements of the Universal code that appear in your physical body and throughout nature. Your fingerprints do not change. Your blood type and DNA are immutable. There is a finite number of eggs or sperm your body will generate in this lifetime. This list continues even to the most diminutive of details still undiscovered by humankind. Yet, we know enough of this design to appreciate that the body is an instrument of Consciousness to pursue our highest good. Patterns are found in everything, from music to molecules.

The spiritual Awakening is not accurately reflected by platitudes or scriptures, and it is not to be memorized and regurgitated in the name of vanity or martyrdom. It is Divine guidance to be understood and *activated* in all your daily encounters to benefit humankind, because all is One. Religions attempt to instill these ideals in believers but fall short by prioritizing rules for the body. *Do this. Don't do that.*

You're a sinner. You're forgiven. You're not worthy. Don't trust other religions. Fear people who believe differently.

In modern society, traditional religious teachings are becoming increasingly unpopular because of the depressing focus on punishment for a sinful nature. This message is received only too well. The actual maturation process of spirituality is in opposition with these beliefs! People have incorporated the doom and gloom of being imperfect beings into everyday life. It no longer holds interest. It has been received over thousands of years and is losing efficacy. It is time to receive the lessons of the Universal Laws that focus more on the amazing grace and perfection the Universe provides to raise the vibration of the world.

Examine how you participate in life. It is incumbent upon you to reconcile your beliefs with the Universal Laws. They are not contradictory (unless, of course, you still believe you are your body).

It is your spirit that is interconnected with everyone you meet or pass on the street. This is why a smile or a kind word from a stranger can brighten your day. In the physical realm, your body is a temple that combines these unique vibrational frequencies and then expresses them in physical form. In spirituality, we recognize the body as a tool. Because all things are connected by the Divine fabric of giving and receiving, the real temple of your spirit is in the relationship to others. This is the nectar connecting all of life. You also know it as love.

Without any effort on your part, your body came into existence by the Universal design that creates through relationship with others. Do not give it more importance than your spirit, which is the highest expression of the Consciousness that is you.

HEALING

A body that is sick is symptomatic of a bigger truth. It reveals the choices of what is consumed, from food to pollution to hateful energy. Do not put faith in the body to heal the body. At this point, you know you have infinite potential to create and attract through your thoughts. Thoughts create outcomes.

Do not limit your healing potential by using the same limited bodily tools. A fire is not extinguished with more fire; it is overcome with water or an element other than itself. Likewise, when a child catches a cold in a house full of children, the mother will often isolate that child to rest and heal and to avoid the spread of sickness throughout the house. The sickness is overcome first by the love and compassion of the mother, who then intercedes for her child by establishing the conditions for rest and healing.

When we focus more on the body than the spirit, we operate illogically. Stop believing that a burnt steak is about the meat; its condition is about the heat that charred it. Adjust the temperature—which is energy—and the condition of the meat will change accordingly. The effect reveals the cause. In this way, as we Awaken, we see our questions are always answered when posed. It is of primary importance, and much more powerful, to utilize the Universal Laws to create the conditions of life. The starting point for healing is to recalibrate the energy that powers the body. Like adjusting the heat to cook the perfect steak, raise your vibration and the body will respond accordingly.

Healing is an energetic vibration of health, which exists in abundance in Consciousness and is your default condition. The world has this backward. You don't have to get healthy; you have to remove the conditions for sickness that you introduce into your daily life. Reorient your understanding of healing to reflect this and put the body into the service of the mind. Healing the flesh is much more than calories consumed and energy expended. Healing, then, is a recalibration of the energy inputs that are powering your life—a tune-up, if you will.

No one asks for sickness, obesity, or death. It is the un-Conscious ego that asks for it and receives it in the body. How? It says, "Eat this fatty, processed food. You deserve it. Drink sugary and alcoholic beverages to dull the vibration of your experiences. Breathe polluted air so you can live in a big city." The buildup of these seemingly independent decisions culminates in sickness.

Wise choices from the power of Consciousness can immediately undo the illusion ego creates. You have been tricked by the human training of your mind to believe that what is not good for you will make you happy, when actually, it makes you sick. When you understand this, the only clear choice that can overcome the subversive nature of the ego is *spirit*. All healing comes from Consciousness's power to defeat the fear of the ego.

So, really think about what you are thinking about. It is your mind that acts first and then expresses itself through your senses. Many of us have forgotten how to use the Universal tools as we are meant to. Sound is a powerful energetic vibration, and this is why words matter. Yet, the true power is the intent that creates the sound. Think of a whisper versus a scream. All intention is born of connection and alignment—energetically and thoughtfully from Consciousness. Awakened decisions bring peace, while un-Conscious decisions wreak havoc, and the body reflects the disfunction physically via disease.

Your condition is never exclusively of your doing. Because we are all One, the collective is a compilation of independent choices affecting everyone. Pollution and food-related sicknesses are results of the collective mind in society at the time. The decision to make cars and create shelf-stable foods can only be supported by your participation. You tacitly participate when you consume processed products or support companies' operations that generate pollution, toxic waste, or any type of sickness as a natural byproduct. These choices are ingested by your body and then passed onto the next generation during the gestation of a fetus. You determine how the world is by how you participate in it. Everything you do matters. It is time to *Awaken*.

The Universe is so abundant that no one need be hungry or without shelter. The ego, being fear based, believes in the illusion of lack, and this misunderstanding breeds hoarding and competition. As you personally participate in this thinking, you also create the conditions for war and atrocities, because everything is connected. The truth is that it is in your own best interests to share rather than hoard, which is demonstrated in all of the Universal Laws, starting with the Law of Giving & Receiving. Take responsibility for your role in healing yourself and the planet, because the world has it backward. Relationships are the true temple of the spirit. Nothing has precedence over compassion for humankind. Love rules.

The energy that courses through our body also courses through every other thing in creation. This energy is where wisdom is extracted from and where our focus is required. The sooner you nurture the inner *you* to lead the choices in your life, the quicker your joy.

Remember, you are not your body; you are so much more. The body is neutral, at best—a tool of communication relaying what the mind has commanded. Start today and let your *mind* commence the healing in your life.

To be, or not to be: that is the question.

Shakespeare, *Hamlet*

A CAUTIONARY TALE

There is a cautionary tale within the story of *Alice's Adventures in Wonderland*. Alice falls down the hole of a white rabbit and ends up in Wonderland. When she falls down the rabbit hole, she enters a strange and absurd alternate universe where space and time are distorted. She grows only to shrink, doorways are the size of mouse holes, and magic is real. She has a tea party with talking animals, enters a garden of live playing cards, and has a variety of other bizarre experiences that were all real to her, at the time. At the end of the story, she wakes up back in Reality, and everything is back to normal.

This story is a classic fairy tale—and a cautionary tale. Humankind is like Alice believing her experience of illusions and dreams in Wonderland is real and forgetting that the true Reality of existence is Consciousness. We are Awakening to that now, like Alice awoke from her dream.

The tendency of humankind is to stay in the comfort of the dream of their own making instead of participating in the ebb and flow of the Universal Laws. We see this clearly in the rising rates of depression, conspiracy theories, and a culture of divisiveness. Unfortunately, this futile attempt ends in misery, because we cannot escape the Laws of the Universe. It is important to Awaken.

In the story, it is what Alice drinks or eats that makes her big or small and sets up the next adventure. Now, imagine that at the end of Alice's dream, she wakes up not to her human reality with her sister but goes even further down the rabbit hole—where she doesn't need to eat or drink to live. She need only put on a pair of glasses and earphones to experience travel and flight and to form an entirely new environment in her vision. Welcome to the Metaverse.

The Metaverse is the vision of a digital reality where human minds will travel, meet, and live virtually through digital holograms and information systems. A prophecy if you will. Artificial intelligence in gaming and entertainment is already creating alternate realities, like in *Alice's Adventures in Wonderland*. The metaverse is not a dream nor a drug-induced state; it is the voluntary pursuit of the fantastic illusory experience instead of the attainment of inner peace in Consciousness. This new technology creates another level of illusion and therefore more trouble for those unacquainted with the Laws of the Universe, because the Metaverse is trip down another level in the proverbial rabbit hole. Temptation threatens the players to embrace the Laws of the Metaverse before equipping themselves with the omni-important Laws of the Universe.

The digital dream is infiltrating life's critical systems. The notion of money is rapidly changing through global digital systems. Cryptocurrency, blockchain, and their digital offspring are becoming commonplace. The digital age is growing, and when nonform digital experiences become the predominant experiences of Consciousness, the body becomes obsolete.

If this seems unrealistic, remember that experiences are a result of sensations and feelings born from thought, and thought is born from mind. If I choose to put on a headset to live in a virtual reality, I am directly connecting my thoughts and perceptions to experiences, and my body need do nothing. Correct?

This fantastic demonstration proves that your body is the container that serves the mind to experience interactions in this world. You are not your body. The digital age is expeditiously teaching us that we can interact mentally without the use of the body and reestablishes the truth that life is a dream born out of the mind of Consciousness.

Still hard to fathom? Before the discovery of sound waves, we could not communicate over long distances. We could be heard only as far as earshot would allow. Then it was discovered that wires and cables could carry sound much farther, and so phones and radios were invented. Then it was discovered, at yet another frequency, that even wires weren't needed. Now, everything is wireless, in the cloud, digital. Everything begins first as a theory until the mind uncovers it. Evolution suggests the hardwired headset will be followed by wireless, nonform solutions. There is another frequency that connects directly to the primordial code embedded in the Universal fabric. It is of the *mind*.

Digital code is built with rules and reason and adheres to the Universal Laws. Evolution also suggests that a virus or antigen will attempt to corrupt the system and continue the ancient battle for the soul of humankind. It is already prevalent in computer viruses, identity theft, and digital warfare via hacking.

Awakening is critical in birthing the Metaverse, or the progress of humankind may be stalled for generations before the pendulum of self-awareness swings back toward enlightenment. We cannot continue to make the mistake of believing the next innovation will bring the peace we seek. Only *Source* can do that. It is important we anchor ourselves in Consciousness, or we risk declining so deeply in the collective amnesia that we pass the point of an already incredibly arduous return.

The body will spend significant time wired into a digital matrix. It is already happening with the barrage of digital social media platforms we tap into constantly. This is no longer science fiction. In just one generation, people transitioned from family gatherings, rituals, and meals together to video conferencing, online learning and shopping, and meal deliveries from phone to porch.

The Universal Laws teach that thought matters most, and thought is what creates Reality. The body is a tool at the behest of thought until perhaps a more advanced tool is created. When you open your mind to the unlimited possibilities of Consciousness, you can imagine that a modified human body or an artificial intelligence being is within the realm of possibility. Lean not into your own understanding but into how the Universe operates. Everything in creation begins in the mind, with a thought.

It is our time to be the light that attracts and Awakens humankind to our own freedom and our direct connection with Consciousness. In this way, we save the body and preserve this playground for life instead of moving on to a different way. If artificial intelligence becomes the real intelligence of the world, it will be because of the choices being made today. Everything matters. The world is a collective Consciousness, and your thoughts, beliefs, and choices matter in its creation.

This is another fascinating aspect of Consciousness experiencing itself: all the Laws of the Universe creating first the world, the oceans, then the land, and finally man and woman; all material things coming from the vibration of Consciousness modulating itself into form. In the new era, the human condition returns to a nonform of energy. Might it be digital?

More importantly, will it be built on a platform of love or fear? Thoughts are units of energy that produce outcomes.

Contemplation: What do you believe? Do you believe in the miraculous and mystical? Are you grounded in Conscious awareness?

PART FOUR

THE WAY

Do you know the laws of the universe and how the heavens influence the earth?

God addressing Job, Job 38:33 (TLB)

AWAKENING: THE SPIRITUAL JOURNEY

The spiritual journey answers life's questions and attunes you with the world around you. The goal is self-discovery and Awakening to your inner nature and the nature of all things. This is the journey in search of the answers to *What is the purpose of everything?* and *Who Am I?* As you Awaken, you see the fullness and richness of life in totality. All the pieces make sense because each is critical to the whole—so much so that they actually don't make any sense separately anymore, like a single hair in a dog's coat or one grain of salt in a saltshaker. The dog would be cold if it weren't for every hair it had to compose its fur, and the saltshaker would be empty if it weren't for every individual grain of salt.

Thus, it's true that every big and small thing serves an individual purpose, but it is the collective purpose it serves that is most important.

Awakening begins with a question.

For instance, a young woman hosts a dinner for her friends. One friend has become particularly versed in matters of the mystical. The hostess, not convinced her friend has any truer knowledge than anyone else, says, "Let me ask you, why do anything at all if there is such an all-knowing and beneficent God? Why pray at all? Why do governments commit atrocities like slavery, holocaust, and war? Why does sickness exist, and how could God allow pandemics? Where is He in times of need?"

The friend quietly takes measure of her hostess. Perhaps the hostess wanted to have fun at her expense rather than deeply explore the truth. However, these questions reveal a ripeness for Awakening, even when unaware. So, the mystic applies the Universal Laws, which should always be consulted as the roadmap to the answers you seek. *Ask, and it is given.*

The mystic replies, "We can have this conversation; however, you must be willing to have an open mind."

The hostess says, "I'm interested in hearing your perspectives." At that intersecting moment of attention, there was a vibrational match between the two women, and a space of agreement was created in Consciousness. The desire to hear and the desire to be heard are the point of attraction and the portal through which understanding occurs. Only the ears that *can* hear *will* hear. This is the beginning point of all reconciliation.

Now, the mystic leans into the Law of Relationship. The mystic's eyes study the designer table mat before her, and she says, "Look at the intricate pattern of this mat. It's like a labyrinth or intersecting tree branches. All things in existence are like the interwoven network of design that exists in this mat. It is the Divine fabric that connects all things. Wherever I am is one point of decision. From a distance, the ego sees chaos and says, 'Follow me. I'll hide you from the rest of the journey.' On this path, fear becomes a self-contained prison.

"Reason, unlike ego, sees a roadmap and says, 'I can find my way forward or backward, left or right. I can take many paths. Some will lead me to where I started, but eventually, with persistence, patience, and perseverance, all roads lead me to freedom. I am secure knowing that I can always, at any moment, choose and choose again the experiences I want to have along the way.'

"Infinite decision tree paths already exist in the mind of the Universe. It is the nature of unlimited possibilities that nothing can be left out. Reality is embedded in the Divine fabric. It is for you to decide how you want to experience life, and *this* choice is your path. This answers the question, 'Why do anything if it is written already?' All paths are known in Consciousness, yet you still choose at every moment which journey is yours to take—the one of joy or of pain.

"The path of least resistance is the one in accordance with the Laws of the Universe. Every instant is informed with the knowledge that is expedient for healing. We are guided to this path from our awareness and understanding of the truth that is greater than the body, as it is of spirit. It is the way of joy accessed through prayer and meditation.

Prayer is a spiritual communication during which you impress your desires into the fabric of the Universe with focused energy. You give your desires to the Universe to attract that which you desire. Meditation is the stillness of the mind; it unclutters your thoughts, making room for Divine guidance to be given by the Universe for your best and highest use. This answers your question, 'Why pray?'

"Negative energy is the resonance of fear. Fearful thoughts create fearful outcomes. When individuals share fears, a new collective mind is created, but this one believes in the illusion of fear and brings with it sickness in behavior and in the body and infects the *collective* body. This is the sickness in governments that commit atrocities against their own citizens. Societies are not the creation of one person. Society, by definition, is a community of people living in close proximity with shared customs and laws. It takes the agreement of a collective mind to share and create or destroy, as revealed by the unbiased Laws of the Universe. Like is drawn to like, and beliefs are the same way—they attract one another, even if they are rooted in sickness and destruction.

"And then we have the collective. Call it a family, a neighborhood, a society, a global order, or a government. Bigotry cannot survive alone in only one man. Societal and class biases reflected in society are the shared collective thoughts of several beings, until a tilting point is reached. These ideas are an attraction point for people who live in the way of fear instead of love. This answers both your questions, 'Why does sickness exist?' and 'Why do governments commit atrocities against human beings?'

"It is also true that love and unity have the opposite effect. Your participation in this Reality changes the reality itself. As we amass enough minds to join and live in the joy and inner peace of the Universal Laws, we change the world to be what it is meant to be. Blaming others for the world's condition does not abdicate you from your responsibility, nor does it change your purpose. The Universal Laws of Awakening function flawlessly, whether you know it or not, and you need to accept their terms.

"It is your function to participate in the healing of the Universe. You dismiss the natural laws and order of the Universe because a situation is not deemed fair by you or to your liking. Do you know better than The Great Author of All That Is? A person who believes they are justified in their grievances and can create a system better than that which knows the All of infinity is like a petulant child. They have a perspective not yet aware of the ways of the world and the journey to enlightenment. It is like going in the opposite direction of your destination and then being angry because you didn't arrive early.

"Learn this one thing and know it well: No peace can be found outside the order of the Universal Laws, no matter how many or how loud the complaints. The petulant child is never happy and suffers under the weight of his own choices—low energy, high stress, and eventually sickness. The same applies to leaders of nations and everyone in between.

"The path of enlightenment does not promise you will enjoy the lessons—quite the contrary. Events must shock you and the collective into awareness if you will not take the responsibility yourself. Unfortunately, the conditioning of suffering and sacrifice has made pain the most effective tool to spur humankind into action. It doesn't have to be this way, but this is the way it is for now.

This is what it means that *all things are working for your good*. Those who believe this create a life of fulfillment and joy in each instant by using the Laws of the Universe to overcome adversity. You can recognize this person by their lightness and loving nature.

"All spiritual traditions teach the principles of the unity of all things and how to bring awareness into the daily practice of a joyful life. You cannot serve two masters. The Universal Laws of Flow, Polarity, Relationship, Vibration, Receiving, and such, are all in service to the One. In fact, they are the fruit of Consciousness, and reveal its truth, like how you recognize a tree by its fruit. The Laws of the Universe are always at play. Consciousness, the One, The Great Author of All That Is, abides where it has always been—in the interspaces of everything, holding up all that is, including your very breath. This answers the question, 'Where is God in my time of need?'"

The hostess feels thankful. The mystic has helped shift her perspectives about the world. Later that night, the hostess has the *Dream of My Box*... and Awakens.

The way of fools seems right to them, but the wise listen to advice.

Proverbs 12:15 (NIV)

PRACTICAL PRACTICES FOR AWAKENING

A man bumps into a female acquaintance at a restaurant and has a short, polite conversation to catch up. She makes a quip about the controversial politics of the day, and he becomes distrustful of her character. He finds himself angry, even hostile toward the woman's political perspectives and begins to recount the story to his friends from a position of moral authority. He remains unsettled even as he, in his own opinion, makes himself right and her wrong.

In frustration, the man goes to his spiritual doula and says, "Give me practical tips on how to ignore small people. I don't want philosophy on how the Universe or God or Consciousness work. I need to know what I can do right here and right now, in the *real* world, to find peace and get this anger out of my heart."

Every spiritual journey encounters this question. It marks the time of *something major* happening in your life. The answer is here, and now you have it. The Laws of the Universe as they govern Reality illuminate the path of least resistance to overcoming any circumstance that befalls you.

The definition of *practical* is doing something rather than being concerned with the ideas behind them. Therefore, the practical activity of doing is secondary. Awareness of the Universal Laws is the primary solution to all problem-solving. Let's approach them in order of importance and priority for your journey of Awakening.

THE SPIRITUAL SCIENTIFIC METHOD

The Universal Laws of Awakening overcome any barriers to a life of happiness and inner peace. Like the industrial and information ages, a new technology is emerging that can change your life and change the world. We are talking about spiritual technology, which is older than the notion of time itself. Instead of diminishing returns, with spiritual technology, we experience the ebb and flow of life, which is infinite and can never be diminished; it expands and contracts, never-ending, *eternal*.

This spiritual technology requires us to detach from past conditionings of guilt and shame and to cling to the Universal Laws that bring happiness. We are evolving. Materiality is an obsolete path to happiness, and continued focus on it may bring riches, but it can certainly bring misery as well. They are not mutually exclusive.

The purpose of all things is to experience life in alignment with the Universal Laws, not to amass material things. Alignment is a constant process of calibration. Your only function is to participate consciously, in a way that makes life enjoyable to you and everyone around you. That only comes with using the Laws of the Universe. Without using these laws, you stray from the center of Conscious awareness, the sense of peace and joy weakens, and the sense of loneliness deepens.

For any problem, and prior to any critical decision or event, use the Spiritual Scientific Method to enliven your Awareness. This practical process will bring clarity, confidence, and transformation, as it activates the Law of Giving & Receiving and navigates you toward the inner peace you desire. You are already familiar with the process but use it for physical research. Open your mind to use it spiritually.

1. Identify the Problem

Ask yourself, "What am I afraid of?" Write down the answer. "I don't know" is not acceptable. The answer is always within you. Start there. Here are examples.

I am an imposter and fear everyone will know.

I am overweight and don't like my body. I do not want people to judge me.

I am unhappy in my relationship and afraid to leave.

I am unhappy being alone and afraid I will never find a partner.

I should have more money to do what I want.

I feel like an outsider to my friends.

I am afraid of leaving this relationship because it will disappoint my friends and family.

2. Hypothesis

Fill in the blank for the following statement to create the theory that you will prove/disprove by using the Universal

Laws. "My fears about ___ indicate what I do *not* want and can be overcome using the lessons from the Laws of the Universe."

3. Observation/Research

Use the Awareness practices of stillness, meditation, breath work, and silence. After this period of preparation, write down how you perceive life and your quality of living. This is a required step in the healing process of Awakening. No progress can happen without this clarifying alignment that comes from introspection and contemplation. Meditate.

4. Experiment

Ask yourself essential questions to apply the Universal Laws to your situation. Use the Contemplations at the end of the Universal Laws chapters to help guide your investigation. Journal your findings.

Is my perspective based on fear or love?
If I had no body, what would I do?
What is this teaching me?
Who am I?
Which Universal Law best serves my understanding?

5. Result

An outcome of inner peace proves the hypothesis. Fear about a specific issue indicates the problem you were seeking to identify in Step 1 of the Spiritual Scientific Method. Begin again with the new problem identified.

6. Conclusion

In all cases, the Spiritual Scientific Method and the Laws of the Universe will bring to you the discovery of some inner wisdom.

Because the Universe is kind and God is benevolent, no one is required to learn but one Universal Law to reach Consciousness. The lesson learned in any one of them can be learned by all of them. You can change your trajectory and recalibrate back to peace at this very moment with any one of the laws because they are Universal. There is beauty in this constant act of renewal and understanding the Universe provides each of us.

The spiritual journey attunes you with the world around you through self-discovery. Awakening to your inner nature allows your potential to shine through and your purpose to emerge.

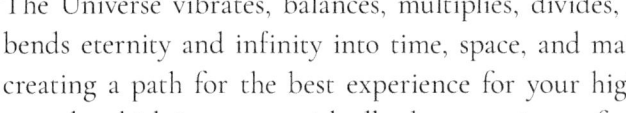

The Universe vibrates, balances, multiplies, divides, and bends eternity and infinity into time, space, and matter, creating a path for the best experience for your highest growth, which intersects with all other experiences for the best outcome of the One. How awesome is the calculation and coordination of creation? The Universal Laws are loving by their impartial application, providing the ultimate justice for any situation.

Where is the threshold of the infinite? We have laws, pathways, energy, and intention to guide the way, but there are no limits to the possibilities in creation. When we choose to follow the Universal Laws of Awakening, we sync up with the energetic life force to restore and change the world.

All the Universal Laws apply to all things, and those versed in these laws live happier lives, as they apply the spiritual technology discussed in this book to transform themselves and the world.

Accept that the course your life is the right path for you. It brought you here. The miracle and beauty of the Universe is that the past, even with all its twists and turns, becomes irrelevant. Regrets are a trite contrivance of the ego. Don't be fooled. In each and every moment, all that matters is choosing the path for your ultimate benefit in the present moment. In this labyrinth of life, you either turn toward love or fear at every point. This path will lead you to the next adventure, in accordance with Universal Laws of order. It is this simple. A choice backed by belief creates the experience in Oneness with all things.

THE SEVEN INTENTIONS

The Spiritual Scientific Method provides a model for problem-solving that is available to everyone. However, if the problem is still too difficult for you to improve your vibration, there are seven "practical" daily intentions you can use to improve your outlook and bring increasing levels of peace. These intentions are based on the Laws of the Universe, and your full understanding is not required for transformation; only your earnest willingness is needed. By practicing these intentions daily for ten days, you Awaken to the Universal Laws. These practical, daily steps accelerate your spiritual growth and purify your body. Solutions are then able to come into your awareness effortlessly. Guidance for this awakening practice is eloquently detailed in *The 10 Days, A Wellness Retreat for personal transformation...at home*. You must know from here on out that even *practical* answers are of God.

1. **Self-Investigation and Meditation:** Go within to stillness and solitude and connect with Consciousness daily. This is critical for confidence and self-assuredness.
2. **Exercise:** Have at least thirty minutes per day of intentional movement to strengthen the body, oxygenate the blood, and keep the vibrational energy centers surrounding the body at their highest vibration for health.
3. **Mindful Eating:** Eat what serves your body and the planet. Do not eat preservatives, refined sugar, or white flour. These clog the body's ability to process information, cause inflammation, and promote sickness and diseases.
4. **Self-Care:** Let kindness and compassion find you. Go beyond luxuriating the body and nurture your Inner Self. Spend time in peaceful places and doing activities where neither guilt nor shame have agency.
5. **Kindness and Gratitude:** Be extraordinarily kind to someone different every day. From strangers to family to pets, it does not matter. Go beyond the common customer service politeness of *Thank You, Please, and Yes Ma'am*. Be generous with your blessings, talents, gifts, and compassion. Help

someone by lifting their spirit. Smile with your eyes. Remember that your vibration can lift the energy of an entire room.

6. **Journaling and Daily Affirmations:** Affirm yourself and all that you are, consciously. *Who am I?* is the essential question to contemplate and on which to journal. *I Am* is the ultimate affirmation.
7. **Rest and Sleep:** Take six to eight hours of sleep or rest each day to let the body rejuvenate. Less time may leave the mind foggy. More time is unnecessary.

These seven intentions are common throughout the world for practical physical and emotional healing. When done daily for ten consecutive days, they raise your vibration so much that you *transform*. Quickly, epiphanies, synchronicities, and ease of effort will be evidence of your Awakening, and your transformation is imminent.

PART FIVE

GO IN PEACE
NEXT STEPS

"It's impossible," said pride.
"It's risky," said experience.
"It's pointless," said reason.
"Give it a try," whispered the heart.

Unknown

Dear Friend,

The purpose of this book is to unpack the Universal Laws, which reveal how all things are connected and guide the way to happiness. The way is simple. It is underscored by the power of *belief*. Thoughts reflect beliefs, and beliefs reveal who you are. You literally become whatever you believe yourself to be, and the Universal Laws facilitate this.

As you Awaken, your thoughts are beginning to naturally perceive life from a mindset of well-being. The victim mentality is obliterated, and you are the master of your life. The world operates differently than how you were conditioned. *The Universal Laws of Awakening* is now a reference guide for understanding how everything works together, how all healing occurs, and how inner peace is attained.

There is a movement of enlightenment afoot. This caste of teachers and believers use the Universal Laws to bring harmony into every situation. You are now a part of that movement. Flow mindfully in the current of grace, just as the Universe intends for you.

May the peace of God be in your awareness always.

Love & Light,
TK

Finally,
be strong in the Lord and in his mighty power.

Put on the full armor of God, so that you can take your stand against the devil's schemes.

For our struggle is not against flesh and blood, but against the rulers, against the authorities, against the powers of this dark world and against the spiritual forces of evil in the heavenly realms.

Therefore put on the full armor of God, so that when evil comes, you may be able to stand your ground, and after you have done everything, to stand.

Ephesians 6:10-14 (NIV)

One Final Note

Dear Reader,

I would love to hear from you.

If you want to share your stories of Awakening, send me a note at TK@RemarkableWellness.us

You can find more practical instruction for the seven Intentions in my book, *The 10 Days: A Wellness Retreat for Personal Transformation...at Home.*

If you seek personal guidance for your spiritual growth, I am a spiritual doula. Join me at:

remarkablewellness.us.

Love & Light,
TK

ACKNOWLEDGEMENTS

First and foremost, I must acknowledge The Great Author of All That Is and sit in gratitude as a unique expression in this wonderful life. I sit in gratitude as a teacher and doula for His wisdom. *Thank you, God.*

Now, I must thank my very patient husband, Craig Stevens, for always supporting me and for loving me so freely. My cup runneth over.

I thank Evan Campbell and Royal Perceptions, LLC for assisting with this project and so many others. He always says yes. My #1 son.

Thank you to Halle Johnstone, my art illustrator, for her bright spirit and for creatively transforming my thoughts into exquisite expressions of God.

Finally, thank you to my friends and family who invested significant time with the Universal Laws and provided substantial insights that improved this work considerably. I love you all: Evan Campbell, Deena Daggett, Sandra McCall, Daryl Minor, and Caitlin Reynolds.

Printed in Dunstable, United Kingdom